MILLAY DELANY

COLLEGE COOKBOOK FOR GUYS

MILLAY DELANY

OVER 60 NO-FUSS AND DORM FRIENDLY RECIPES THAT FIT YOUR BUDGET, FOR BUSY STUDENTS AND MEN TO SATISFY CAMPUS CRAVINGS, AND FUEL YOUR BRAIN

COPYRIGHT

© 2023 by Millay Delany

All rights reserved. No part of this book may be reproduced, stored in a retrieval system, or transmitted in any form or by any means, electronic, mechanical, photocopying, recording, scanning, or otherwise, except as permitted under Section 107 or 108 of the 1976 United States Copyright Act, without the prior written permission of the publisher.

Cover design by Gabriel Chuks
Interior design by Ucee Dezigns

Printed in USA

This book is a guide to easy and practical cooking aimed at college guys. The recipes and tips provided are intended for educational and informational purposes. The author and publisher are not responsible for any adverse effects or consequences resulting from the use of the information in this book. Readers are encouraged to consult with professionals regarding specific dietary needs or concerns.

For permissions, please contact
dietwithmillaydelany@gmail.com.

ACKNOWLEDGMENT

Hello, dear readers,

This cookbook has been a labor of love, and I couldn't have done it without the incredible support and encouragement from those around me. There are a few special people I'd like to extend my heartfelt thanks to.

To my amazing friends who have been by my side through thick and thin—thank you for enduring countless taste tests, offering valuable feedback, and being a constant source of inspiration. Your unwavering support means the world to me, and your enthusiasm for my culinary adventures has fueled my passion for cooking.

A massive shout out to the mentors and educators at the University of Georgia. Your guidance and expertise have shaped my understanding of nutrition and empowered me to share my knowledge through this cookbook.

I want to express my deepest appreciation to the wonderful team at Emeralds Publishing Company. Your dedication, patience, and belief in this project have turned my culinary dreams into a tangible reality. Special thanks to Sonia for her invaluable insights and guidance throughout this journey.

And to all of you diving into these pages, eager to explore and create in your own kitchen—thank you! I hope these recipes bring joy and deliciousness to your table. Your enthusiasm for good food motivates me to continue sharing my culinary experiences.

Warm regards and happy cooking,

Millay Delany

ABOUT THE AUTHOR

Hey, foodie friends!

I'm Millay Delany, your go-to nutrition guru and all-around food enthusiast from the University of Georgia. I'm the kind of person who gets super pumped about creating yummy dishes and making nutrition a blast! When I'm not geeking out over the latest food trends, you'll catch me wandering through farmers' markets or debating with myself (and anyone who'll listen) about why peanut butter rocks my world.

My journey into the world of nutrition kicked off with this burning desire to help folks fall head over heels in love with good food while keeping their health in check. Trust me, college life wasn't just textbooks and lectures for me; it was a whirlwind of cooking experiments, dorm room culinary hacks, and a whole lot of tasty trial and error.

With my book "College Cookbook for Guys," I'm dishing out easy-peasy recipes designed specifically for you college guys out there. I want to make your mealtime stress-free, budget-friendly, and most importantly, delicious! And when I'm not scribbling down recipes, you'll find me in my own kitchen, stirring up some magic or brainstorming my next foodie adventure.

Hungry for more of my culinary wisdom and lip-smacking recipes? Dive into my other works on Amazon.com for a sneak peek behind the scenes!

Let's cook up some awesome dishes together!

Millay Delany

My Grocery List

PANTRY ITEMS

FRUIT & VEGETABLES

MEAT & SEAFOOD

HOME SUPPLIES

CONTENTS

COPYRIGHT	3
ACKNOWLEDGMENT	4
ABOUT THE AUTHOR	5
CUSTOM GROCERY LIST	6

KITCHEN MASTERY 101: THE GUY'S GUIDE TO COOKING

Eat, Impress, Succeed	9
Navigating the Bachelor's Kitchen	11

SETTING UP YOUR BACHELOR KITCHEN

	14
Cooking Hacks Every Guy Should Know	16
Budget-Friendly Strategies	18
Smart Grocery Shopping Tips	

TASTY CAMPUS RECIPES & MEAL PLANNERS

Rise & Shine Breakfast	21
Main Course Marvels	27
Sides Dishes	33
Soups & Stews Showdown	39
Salad Sensations	45
Snack Attack Extravaganza	51
Decadent Dessert Delights	57
Fish & Seafood Fiesta	63
Poultry & Beef Perfection	69
Duck, Lamb, & Pork Palooza	75
Smoothie Sensations	81
Veggie Ventures	87
Sauces, Dips & Dressings	93

CONCLUSION	101

7

PART 1: KITCHEN MASTERY 101: THE GUY'S GUIDE TO COOKING

INTRODUCTION
EAT · IMPRESS · SUCCEED

There was this awesome young dude, called Jake, who was all set to embark on his thrilling journey to college. Yes, that's my nephew! Now, Jake's mom, a marvelous cook, was fretting over her dear boy's upcoming adventure. Why, you ask? Well, Jake had an insatiable appetite for delicious, homemade meals, but let's just say his kitchen skills were pretty much non-existent. The lad could barely tell a spatula from a ladle – that's how dire the situation was!

His Mom was a beacon of concern. Worried that her dear son would subsist solely on microwave noodles and questionable takeout, she sought my culinary expertise. She knew I could whip up something magical, something that would rescue her boy from the realm of culinary disaster. And rescue him, I did!

So, I brewed up a magical concoction of recipes fit for a college hero like Jake. These weren't just any recipes; they were the kind that turned Jake into a kitchen rock star! With these culinary spells, he not only impressed his buddies with scrumptious homemade meals but also swept his crush off her feet with a cozy dinner cooked straight from the heart.

But that's not all, folks! These recipes were more than just tasty – they were brain food, keeping Jake fueled up and ready to conquer his studies like a boss. That's right, these meals weren't just about satisfying hunger; they were about unlocking potential.

Importance? Oh, it's crucial, my friends! Think about it: homemade meals that are easy, quick, and wallet-friendly. If you're a college guy navigating your way through the maze of a bachelor's kitchen, listen up! This book isn't just a collection of recipes; it's your ultimate guide to kitchen survival.

It's your secret weapon to impressing your pals, wooing that special someone with a homemade feast, and keeping your brain in top-notch shape for those intense study sessions.

Inside these pages, you'll find breakfast delights to kickstart your day, veggies that even your mom would approve of, brain-boosting smoothies, epic snacks for those gaming nights, sides that steal the show, main dishes fit for a king, and so much more. And here's the kicker – it's all mom-approved! Yep, your mom would be thrilled to know you're nourishing yourself with these wholesome, easy-to-make meals.

So, buckle up, my friends! It's time to dive into a world where cooking isn't just a chore but an epic adventure waiting to happen. This isn't just a cookbook; it's your secret weapon to conquering the college kitchen like a boss!

NAVIGATING THE BACHELOR'S KITCHEN

Navigating the bachelor's kitchen? It's like mastering a new game level! Let's map out the secrets to mastering the bachelor's kitchen!

First things first, embrace simplicity. We're talking easy-peasy recipes that don't require a Ph.D. in cooking. Think of your kitchen as a playground—experiment, explore, and don't be afraid to make mistakes.

Next up, gear up your kitchen arsenal. Stock your pantry with essentials like pasta, rice, spices, canned goods, and, of course, the superhero of all ingredients—garlic. Trust me, it's a game-changer.

Now, let's talk tools. You don't need a fancy kitchen gadget gadgetry. Just arm yourself with the basics—a reliable pan, a sturdy pot, a good knife, and a cutting board. Oh, and don't forget the trusty microwave for those lightning-fast meals.

Meal planning & prepping is your best friend. Set aside some time to jot down a weekly menu. Plan simple recipes that use similar ingredients to save time and money. It'll save you from those last-minute meal panics and those emergency calls to your local pizza joint.

Learn basic cooking techniques—sautéing, boiling, baking. They're your combat skills in the kitchen! Mastering these moves will let you conquer any recipe. Sometimes quests go awry. Don't panic! Improvise with what you have. Substitutions and tweaks are your secret weapons.

Experimentation is key. Learn your ingredients' strengths and weaknesses, like a character's special abilities! Don't be afraid to tweak recipes or add your own spin. Fresh produce, grains, and lean proteins are your allies.

Experiment, mix, and match to discover flavor combos that'll have you winning every meal. Sometimes, the most mouthwatering discoveries come from happy accidents in the kitchen.

Last but not least, clean as you go. Trust me on this one; a tidy kitchen is a happy kitchen. Plus, it'll save you from facing Mount Dishes later.

With a dash of creativity, a sprinkle of courage, and a pinch of kitchen know-how, you'll navigate the bachelor's kitchen like a seasoned pro. Happy cooking, my friends!

CHAPTER 1
SETTING UP YOUR BACHELOR KITCHEN

Alright, fellas, let's get real about kitchen essentials! We're not talking about fancy gadgets or snazzy gizmos that'll gather dust in a corner. No sir, we're diving into the must-haves for any dude ready to conquer the kitchen.

First up, knives! You need a trusty set—nothing too fancy, just a couple of good-quality knives that'll chop, slice, and dice like a dream. You should get a chef's knife for slicing and dicing, a paring knife for those intricate tasks, and maybe a serrated one for slicing bread like a pro. Trust me, they're your kitchen sidekicks.

Next on the list: pots and pans. Invest in a solid skillet for frying up eggs or searing some meat, a saucepan for sauces and soups, a reliable non-stick pan for those omelettes, and a sturdy pot. These bad boys will have your back when you're whipping up anything from omelettes to pasta to that secret chili recipe. If you can swing it, a decent-quality baking sheet will open up a whole world of crispy goodness for you.

Speaking of baking, don't forget a mixing bowl or two. These babies will be your companions for whipping up batters, tossing salads, and mixing marinades. And let's not overlook the spatula, tongs, and wooden spoons – your kitchen superheroes for flipping, stirring, and serving up those delicious creations.

You should also invest in some food storage containers. These champs will keep your leftovers fresh and tidy up your fridge in style.

Spices, my friends, are your flavor superheroes. Stock up on the essentials—salt, pepper, garlic powder, cumin, paprika, and chili powder. They'll transform your dishes from bland to grand in seconds.

Now, let's talk about the pantry pantry. Keep it stocked with essentials like pasta, rice, canned beans, and tomato sauce. They're the backbone of countless easy, tasty meals.
Measuring cups and spoons are your best pals in the kitchen. They'll help you nail those recipes with precision. Oh, and if you're feeling a bit techy, an electronic scale is a game-changer. It'll ensure accuracy in your measurements and have you baking like a wizard.

Don't forget your fridge allies! Eggs, cheese, butter, and some veggies like onions, bell peppers, and spinach will turn any dull dish into a flavor-packed extravaganza.

And last but not least, the cleaning brigade. Dish soap, sponges, and kitchen towels—because let's face it, no one likes a dirty kitchen.

Alright, gents, these essentials will set you up for kitchen greatness. They're your secret weapons in the battle against hunger. So gear up, stock your kitchen armory, and get ready to cook up a storm!

Cooking Hacks Every Guy Should Know

Alright, lads, listen up! I'm about to drop some serious kitchen wisdom—cooking hacks that'll make you look like a culinary wizard without breaking a sweat.

First off, let's tackle the notorious onion tears. Wanna chop onions without turning into a sobbing mess? Pop 'em in the freezer for 15 minutes before slicing. Voilà! Tears? Nah, not today.

Ever over-salted a dish? Don't panic! Toss in a few potato chunks—they're like flavor sponges, soaking up that excess salt without any fuss.

Speaking of potatoes, wanna make 'em crispy without a fryer? Soak those potato slices in cold water for a bit before frying or roasting. Hello, crispy goodness!

Let's talk about the power of seasoning. Ever heard of the "pinch and taste" method? It's your secret weapon to nail the perfect flavor. Sprinkle a bit of seasoning, taste, adjust. Repeat until your taste buds do a happy dance.

Speaking of seasoning, frozen herbs are your best pals. No more wilted basil or sad parsley—freeze 'em in olive oil in an ice cube tray. Boom! Instant flavor bombs for your dishes.

Let's talk about eggs. To check if an egg is fresh, just plop it in a bowl of water. If it sinks and lays flat, it's fresh as a daisy. If it stands on one end, it's getting there. And if it floats? Well, it's time to say goodbye, my friend.

You know that stubborn jar lid that refuses to budge? Enter your superhero—rubber bands! Wrap one around the lid for a better grip and twist that jar open like a pro.

Oh, the wonders of parchment paper! Line your baking sheets with this magic stuff for easy cleanup. No more scrubbing pans till your arms ache.

Ever struggled with sticky measuring cups? Here's the trick: spray 'em with a bit of cooking oil before measuring sticky stuff like honey or peanut butter. It'll slide right out, no scraping required.

Got stale bread? Don't toss it! Sprinkle some water on it and pop it in the oven for a few minutes. Boom! Fresh-ish bread!

Ran out of a rolling pin? No worries! Grab a wine bottle (empty or full; your call) and roll that dough out like a pro.

Here's one for the microwave masters: place a damp paper towel over leftovers when reheating in the microwave. It keeps things moist and prevents that dreaded rubbery texture.

Lastly, frozen meat got ya down? Run it under cold water while in a sealed plastic bag. It'll thaw faster than you can say "dinner time."

Alright, gents, these cooking hacks are your secret weapons. Embrace 'em, use 'em, and soon you'll be the kitchen guru your friends turn to for culinary wisdom.

Budget-Friendly Strategies

Alright, lads, let's head into the art of cooking on a budget! Who says tasty meals need to break the bank? Not on our watch! Here are some savvy strategies to keep your stomach and wallet equally happy.

First things first—meal planning is your golden ticket. Take a few moments to plan out your week's meals. This way, you'll shop smarter, waste less, and avoid those impulse buys that drain your wallet.

Next up, embrace the wonders of leftovers. Cook big batches and repurpose them throughout the week. That pot of chili you made? Boom, it's now taco filling, chili cheese fries, and maybe even a pasta sauce.

Get cozy with your freezer. Leftovers or extra portions? Freeze 'em! Extra veggies? Freeze 'em! That way, nothing goes to waste, and you've got a stash of meals ready for a rainy (or busy) day. Plus, it prevents food waste and saves you from ordering pricey takeout.

Frozen veggies to the rescue! They're not just budget-friendly but also super convenient. Stock up on frozen peas, broccoli, or mixed veggies to add some nutritional pizzazz to your meals without draining your wallet.

And speaking of veggies, don't ignore the ugly ducklings! Those slightly bruised or odd-shaped produce items are often cheaper and taste just as delicious in your meals.

Bulk buying isn't just for superheroes; it's for budget-savvy cooks too! Hit up those bulk sections at the store for grains, beans, and spices. Buying in bulk saves you a pretty penny in the long run. Sales and discounts are your pals. Keep an eye out for deals on meat or veggies, then freeze or cook in bulk.

Incase you don't know, store brands are your unsung heroes. They're often just as good as name brands but kinder to your wallet. Trust me, your taste buds won't even notice the difference.

Now, let's talk about the magic of versatility. Choose ingredients that can wear multiple hats. Take rice, for example. It's the chameleon of the kitchen—pair it with veggies, toss it in a stir-fry, or use it as a base for a budget-friendly risotto.

Let's talk about the magical world of dry goods. Beans, rice, pasta—these budget-friendly staples are your kitchen knights in shining armor. They're versatile, filling, and won't cost you an arm and a leg.

And last but certainly not least, embrace the art of DIY. Make your own sauces, dressings, and even snacks. They're not just tastier but also way cheaper than their store-bought counterparts.

Alright, gents, these budget-friendly strategies are your golden tickets to delicious meals without draining your bank account. With a bit of planning, creativity, and smart shopping, you'll be ruling the kitchen without blowing your budget. Cheers to good eats and smart spending!

Smart Grocery Shopping Tips

Mastering the art of smart grocery shopping is the secret sauce to conquering the kitchen. Here are some savvy tips to help you navigate those aisles like a pro and save those hard-earned bucks!

First off, come prepared with a plan. Make a list and stick to it! This keeps you focused and stops those pesky impulse buys that sneakily empty your wallet.

Next, the golden rule—never shop hungry. Seriously, it's a trap! You'll end up tossing everything into your cart, , and most likely, things you don't need, and your wallet will weep. Eat beforehand to keep those impulse buys in check.

Let's talk about the power of comparison. Check those prices—store brands versus name brands, different sizes, or bulk options. Sometimes, a little comparison dance can save you a ton!

Now, here's a sneaky trick—shop the perimeter of the store. That's where the fresh produce, dairy, and meats usually hang out. It's healthier and often cheaper than the processed stuff in the aisles.

Produce paradise! Opt for seasonal fruits and veggies—they're usually fresher and cheaper. Plus, frozen veggies are your wallet's best friend and just as nutritious as fresh ones.

The wonders of the freezer aisle! Buying frozen goods in bulk can save you money, and they'll last longer. Think frozen meats, veggies, and even bread—your wallet will thank you.

It's all about the deals, sir! Keep an eye on those sales, discounts, and coupons. Keep an eye out for those yellow stickers and BOGO deals. Stock up on non-perishables or freeze extra portions. They're your ticket to savings and might inspire some creative cooking adventures.

Size matters, gents! No, not that—package size. Sometimes, buying in bulk is cost-effective, but not always. Check the unit price to make sure you're getting the best bang for your buck.

Lastly, don't let expiration dates scare you! Often, items on sale are nearing their expiration date but are perfectly fine to eat. Just plan to use them soon after purchase.

Alright, gents, these smart grocery shopping tips are your key to unlocking kitchen savings. So arm yourself with that list, shop smart, and watch those savings stack up while filling your kitchen with culinary delights! Happy shopping and cooking!

PART 2: TASTY CAMPUS RECIPES

CHAPTER 2
RISE & SHINE BREAKFAST

Chickwizz Sandwich

🍴 2 servings   🕐 10 minutes

INGREDIENTS

- 1 can (160g) of canned chicken (drained)
- 4 tablespoons (60g) mayonnaise
- 2 tablespoons (30g) chopped celery
- 1 tablespoon (15g) chopped onion
- 1 teaspoon (5ml) lemon juice
- Salt and pepper to taste
- 4 slices of bread
- Lettuce leaves and tomato slices for serving

DIRECTIONS

1. In a mixing bowl, combine the drained canned chicken, mayonnaise, chopped celery, chopped onion, lemon juice, salt, and pepper. Mix well.

2. Toast the bread slices lightly, if desired.

3. Divide the chicken mixture evenly between two slices of bread. Top each with lettuce leaves and tomato slices, if preferred. Close the sandwiches with the remaining slices of bread.

4. Serve the Chickwizz Sandwiches immediately and enjoy!

(per serving): Calories: 320 kcal, 0g, Proteins: 25g, Fats: 15g

Peanut Butter Banana Toast

2 servings | 10 minutes

INGREDIENTS

- 4 slices of bread
- 4 tablespoons (60g) peanut butter
- 2 ripe bananas
- Honey (optional, for drizzling)

DIRECTIONS

1. Toast the bread slices until golden brown, either in a toaster or on a skillet over medium heat.

2. Spread 2 tablespoons of peanut butter evenly onto each slice of toasted bread.

3. Peel the bananas and slice them thinly.

4. Place the banana slices on top of the peanut butter-covered toast.

5. Optionally, drizzle a bit of honey over the bananas for added sweetness.

6. Serve the Peanut Butter Banana Toast immediately and enjoy!

(per serving): Calories: 350 kcal, 48g, Proteins: 9g, Fats: 16g

Curry Beans on Toast

🍴 2 servings 🕐 20 minutes

INGREDIENTS

- 1 can (400g/14 oz) of cooked beans (e.g., kidney beans, black beans)
- 1 onion, finely chopped
- 2 cloves of garlic, minced
- 1 tablespoon vegetable oil
- 2 tablespoons curry powder
- 1 can (400g/14 oz) of chopped tomatoes
- Salt and pepper, to taste
- 4 slices of whole grain bread, toasted
- Fresh cilantro or parsley for garnish (optional)

DIRECTIONS

1. Heat the vegetable oil in a pan over medium heat. Add the chopped onion and garlic, sauté until softened.

2. Stir in the curry powder and cook for another minute to release the flavors.

3. Add the chopped tomatoes and cooked beans to the pan. Simmer for about 10 minutes, stirring occasionally, until the sauce thickens.

4. Season with salt and pepper to taste.

5. While the beans are simmering, toast the slices of whole grain bread.

6. Once the beans are done, spoon the curry beans over the toasted bread.

7. Garnish with fresh cilantro or parsley if desired.

8. Serve hot and enjoy your hearty Curry Beans on Toast!

(per serving): Calories: 380 kcal, 50g, Proteins: 18g, Fats: 7g

Cheesy Bacon Breakfast Burrito

🍴 2 servings   🕐 25 minutes

INGREDIENTS

- 4 slices of bacon, chopped (113 g)
- 4 large eggs
- 1/4 cup (60 ml) milk
- Salt and pepper to taste
- 1/2 cup (60 g) shredded cheddar cheese
- 2 large flour tortillas
- Salsa or hot sauce (optional)
- Chopped fresh cilantro or green onions for garnish (optional)

DIRECTIONS

1. In a skillet over medium heat, cook the chopped bacon until crispy. Remove the bacon from the skillet and set aside, leaving the bacon grease in the pan.

2. In a bowl, whisk together the eggs, milk, salt, and pepper until well combined.

3. Pour the egg mixture into the skillet with the bacon grease. Cook, stirring occasionally, until the eggs are scrambled and just set. Remove from heat.

4. Divide the shredded cheese between the tortillas, spreading it evenly down the center of each tortilla.

5. Spoon the scrambled eggs onto the cheese on each tortilla, then sprinkle the cooked bacon on top.

6. Optionally, add salsa or hot sauce for extra flavor. Roll up each tortilla, folding in the sides, to create two burritos.

7. Return the burritos to the skillet over medium-low heat and cook for 2-3 minutes on each side until they are golden and crispy.

8. Garnish with chopped cilantro or green onions if desired.

(per serving):, Calories: 540 kcal, 23g, Protein: 27g, Fat: 36g

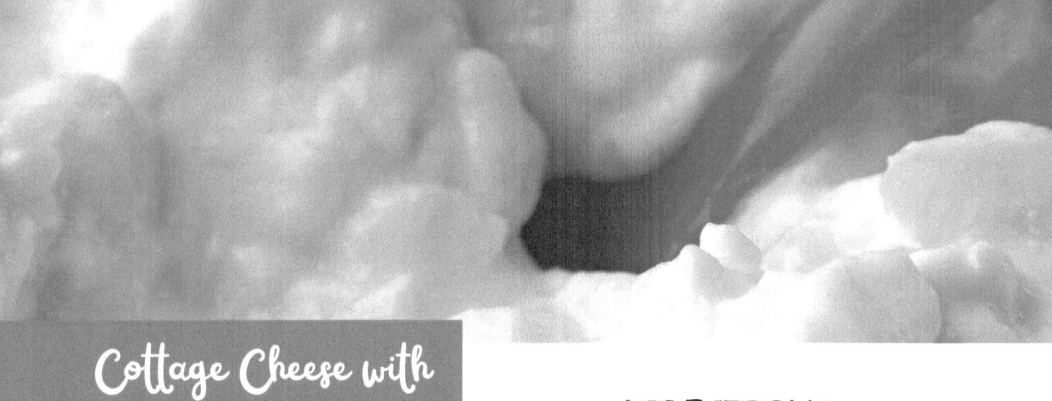

Cottage Cheese with Pineapple Chunks

🍴 2 servings 🕒 5 minutes

INGREDIENTS

- 500 g (2 cups) cottage cheese
- 400 g (1 3/4 cups) fresh pineapple chunks
- 30 ml (2 tablespoons) honey (optional)
- A handful (30) of chopped nuts (optional)
- A dash of cinnamon (optional)

DIRECTIONS

1. Divide the cottage cheese equally into two serving bowls.

2. Top each bowl of cottage cheese with half of the fresh pineapple chunks.

3. Drizzle a tablespoon of honey over each bowl for added sweetness if desired.

4. Optionally, sprinkle each bowl with a handful of chopped nuts for extra crunch and a dash of cinnamon for flavor.

5. Mix lightly if preferred and enjoy!

serving): Calories: 380 kcal, 35g, Proteins: 40g, Fats: 7g

MY WEEKLY MEAL PLANNER

Monday

Tuesday

Wednesday

Thursday

Friday

Saturday

Sunday

CHAPTER 3
MAIN COURSE MARVELS

Speedy Chicken Alfredo

🍴 2 servings   🕐 30 minutes

INGREDIENTS

- 200g fettuccine pasta (7 ounces)
- 2 boneless, skinless chicken breasts (300g or 10.5 ounces)
- 2 tablespoons (30 ml) olive oil
- 2 cloves garlic, minced
- 1 cup heavy cream (240ml)
- 1 cup grated Parmesan cheese (100g)
- Salt and pepper to taste
- Chopped parsley for garnish (optional)

DIRECTIONS

1. Cook the fettuccine pasta according to package instructions. Drain and set aside.

2. Cut the chicken breasts into bite-sized pieces. Season with salt and pepper.

3. In a large skillet over medium-high heat, add olive oil. Cook the chicken pieces until browned and fully cooked, around 5-6 minutes. Remove from the skillet and set aside.

4. In the same skillet, add minced garlic and cook for 1 minute until fragrant.

5. Reduce the heat to low. Pour in the heavy cream and stir until it starts to simmer.

6. Gradually add the grated Parmesan cheese, stirring continuously until the sauce thickens and the cheese is melted.

7. Add the cooked chicken pieces back into the skillet with the sauce. Stir to combine and cook for an additional 2-3 minutes.

8. Add the cooked fettuccine pasta to the skillet. Toss until the pasta is well coated with the sauce.

9. Serve the Speedy Chicken Alfredo hot, garnished with chopped parsley if desired.

Nutritional Information (per serving): Calories: 780, Carbohydrates: 45g, Proteins: 42g, Fats: 47g

Tantalizing Beef Stir-Fry

🍴 2 servings 🕐 25 minutes

INGREDIENTS

- 300g (10.5 oz) beef sirloin, thinly sliced
- 2 tablespoons (30 ml) vegetable oil
- 2 cups (480 ml) mixed vegetables (bell peppers, broccoli, carrots)
- 3 cloves garlic, minced
- 2 tablespoons (30 ml) soy sauce
- 1 tablespoon (15 ml) oyster sauce
- 1 tablespoon (15 ml) cornstarch
- 1 teaspoon (5 ml) sesame oil

DIRECTIONS

1. In a bowl, mix the sliced beef with soy sauce, oyster sauce, cornstarch, and sesame oil. Let it marinate for 10 minutes.

2. Heat vegetable oil in a large skillet or wok over medium-high heat. Add minced garlic and stir-fry for 30 seconds until fragrant.

3. Add the marinated beef to the skillet. Stir-fry for 2-3 minutes until browned.

4. Add mixed vegetables to the skillet and continue stir-frying for an additional 3-4 minutes until the vegetables are tender yet crisp.

5. Serve the beef stir-fry over cooked rice or noodles.

(per serving): Calories: 420 kcal, 0g, Proteins: 30g, Fats: 25g

Taco Bowl

🍴 2 servings   🕐 30 minutes

INGREDIENTS

- 1 cup cooked rice (200g)
- 1 tablespoon cooking oil (15ml)
- 1/2 lb ground beef (225g)
- 1/2 cup black beans, drained and rinsed (120g)
- 1/2 cup corn kernels (90g)
- 1/2 teaspoon chili powder (2.5g)
- 1/2 teaspoon cumin powder (2.5g)
- Salt and pepper to taste
- 1 cup shredded lettuce (60g)
- 1/2 cup diced tomatoes (100g)
- 1/4 cup shredded cheddar cheese (30g)
- Optional toppings: sliced jalapeños, diced avocado, sour cream

DIRECTIONS

1. Cook rice according to package instructions. Set aside.

2. Heat oil in a skillet over medium heat. Add ground beef and cook until browned, breaking it apart with a spatula as it cooks.

3. Drain excess fat from the skillet. Add black beans, corn, chili powder, cumin powder, salt, and pepper. Stir and cook for 3-4 minutes until heated through.

4. Assemble the bowls: Divide the cooked rice between two bowls. Top with the beef mixture, shredded lettuce, diced tomatoes, shredded cheddar cheese, and any optional toppings you desire.

5. Serve immediately and enjoy your hearty Taco Bowls!

(per serving): Calories: 550 kcal, 50g, Protein: 28g, Fat: 25g

Egg Fried Rice

🍴 2 servings   🕒 30 minutes

INGREDIENTS

- 1 cup (185g) uncooked white rice
- 2 eggs
- 2 tablespoons vegetable oil
- 1/2 cup (75g) diced carrots
- 1/2 cup (75g) frozen peas
- 2 tablespoons soy sauce
- Salt and pepper to taste
- Optional: chopped green onions for garnish

DIRECTIONS

1. Cook rice according to package instructions. Once cooked, allow it to cool completely.

2. In a bowl, beat the eggs and season with a pinch of salt and pepper.

3. Heat 1 tablespoon of vegetable oil in a large skillet or wok over medium-high heat.

4. Pour the beaten eggs into the skillet and scramble them. Once cooked, remove them from the skillet and set aside.

5. In the same skillet, heat the remaining tablespoon of oil. Add the diced carrots and frozen peas. Stir-fry for 3-4 minutes until the veggies are tender.

6. Add the cooled rice to the skillet with the vegetables. Stir-fry for another 2-3 minutes.

7. Pour the soy sauce over the rice and vegetables. Mix well to combine.

8. Finally, add the scrambled eggs back into the skillet. Stir-fry for an additional 1-2 minutes until everything is heated through.

9. Adjust seasoning with additional salt and pepper if needed. Optionally, garnish with chopped green onions before serving.

(per serving): Calories: 420 kcal, 5g, Proteins: 14g, Fats: 16g

One-Pot Chili Mac

🍴 2 servings   🕐 30 minutes

INGREDIENTS

- 225g (8 oz) ground beef
- 1 small onion, diced
- 2 cloves garlic, minced
- 1 can (400g/14 oz) diced tomatoes
- 1 cup (250ml) beef broth
- 1 cup (250ml) water
- 1 cup (150g) elbow macaroni
- 1 teaspoon chili powder
- 1 teaspoon paprika
- 1/2 teaspoon cumin
- Salt and pepper to taste
- 1 cup (115g) shredded cheddar cheese

DIRECTIONS

1. In a large skillet or pot over medium heat, brown the ground beef with diced onions and minced garlic until the beef is no longer pink and the onions are translucent, around 5-7 minutes. Drain excess fat if needed.

2. Stir in the diced tomatoes, beef broth, water, elbow macaroni, chili powder, paprika, cumin, salt, and pepper. Bring the mixture to a boil.

3. Reduce the heat to a simmer and cover the pot. Let it cook for about 12-15 minutes, stirring occasionally, until the macaroni is cooked through and most of the liquid is absorbed.

4. Sprinkle the shredded cheddar cheese over the top, cover, and let it sit for a few minutes until the cheese melts.

5. Serve hot and enjoy your hearty One-Pot Chili Mac!

(per serving): Calories: 560 kcal, 9g, Proteins: 32g, Fats: 30g

MY WEEKLY MEAL PLANNER

Monday

Tuesday

Wednesday

Thursday

Friday

Saturday

Sunday

CHAPTER 4
SIDES DISHES

Creamy Mac and Cheese

🍴 2 servings 🕐 20 minutes

INGREDIENTS

- 200g (7 oz) elbow macaroni
- 2 cups (500ml) water
- 1/2 cup (120ml) milk
- 1 cup (115g) shredded cheddar cheese
- 1 tablespoon (14g) butter
- Salt and pepper to taste

DIRECTIONS

1. In a pot, bring water to a boil. Add a pinch of salt and elbow macaroni. Cook according to package instructions until al dente.

2. Drain the cooked macaroni and return it to the pot. Place the pot over low heat.

3. Add milk, shredded cheddar cheese, butter, salt, and pepper to the cooked macaroni. Stir continuously until the cheese melts and forms a creamy sauce.

4. Continue to cook for a few more minutes until the sauce thickens and coats the macaroni.

5. Remove from heat and let it sit for a couple of minutes to thicken further.

6. Serve hot and enjoy your indulgent Creamy Mac and Cheese!

(per serving): Calories: 550 kcal, 5g, Proteins: 22g, Fats: 26g

Loaded Nachos

🍴 2 servings   🕐 20 minutes

INGREDIENTS

- 200g (7 oz) tortilla chips
- 200g (7 oz) ground beef
- 1 cup (115g) shredded cheddar cheese
- 1/2 cup (75g) black beans, drained and rinsed
- 1/2 cup (60g) diced tomatoes
- 1/4 cup (30g) sliced jalapeños (adjust to taste)
- 1/4 cup (30g) diced red onion
- 1/4 cup (30g) sliced black olives
- 1/4 cup (30g) chopped fresh cilantro
- 1/2 teaspoon chili powder
- 1/2 teaspoon cumin
- Salt and pepper to taste

DIRECTIONS

1. Preheat the oven to 375°F (190°C).

2. In a skillet over medium heat, cook the ground beef until browned. Drain excess fat if needed. Add chili powder, cumin, salt, and pepper for seasoning.

3. On a baking sheet or oven-safe dish, spread out the tortilla chips evenly.

4. Sprinkle half of the shredded cheddar cheese over the chips. Then layer with cooked ground beef, black beans, diced tomatoes, jalapeños, red onion, and black olives. Top with the remaining shredded cheddar cheese.

5. Bake in the preheated oven for about 8-10 minutes, or until the cheese is melted and bubbly.

6. Remove from the oven and sprinkle fresh cilantro on top.

7. Serve immediately. Serve loaded nachos with fresh guacamole and salsa, cilantro-lime crema, a simple garden salad, Caesar salad, or rice and beans. Enjoy your generous serving of Loaded Nachos!

(per serving): Calories: 800 kcal, 4g, Proteins: 35g, Fats: 50g

Caprese Stuffed Avocado

🍴 2 servings   🕐 10 minutes

INGREDIENTS

- 2 ripe avocados
- 240 ml (1 cup) cherry tomatoes, halved
- 113 grams (4 ounces) fresh mozzarella cheese, diced
- Fresh basil leaves, torn
- Balsamic glaze, for drizzling
- Salt and pepper, to taste

DIRECTIONS

1. Cut the avocados in half and remove the pits. Scoop out a bit of avocado flesh from each half to create a larger cavity.

2. In a bowl, combine the cherry tomatoes, diced fresh mozzarella, and torn basil leaves. Season with salt and pepper to taste.

3. Stuff each avocado half generously with the tomato, mozzarella, and basil mixture.

4. Drizzle balsamic glaze over the stuffed avocados.

5. Serve immediately. This Caprese Stuffed Avocado can be served as a stand-alone dish for a light meal or as a side dish alongside grilled chicken, fish, or a mixed green salad for a more complete and filling meal. Enjoy your hearty Caprese Stuffed Avocado!

(per serving): Calories: 300 kcal, 5g, Proteins: 12g, Fats: 25g

Sesame Ginger Green Beans

🍴 2 servings   🕐 15 minutes

INGREDIENTS

- 250 g (9 ounces) fresh green beans, ends trimmed
- 15 ml (1 tablespoon) sesame oil
- 2 cloves garlic, minced
- 5 g (1 teaspoon) grated ginger
- 15 ml (1 tablespoon) soy sauce
- 5 ml (1 teaspoon) honey
- 5 g (1 teaspoon) sesame seeds
- Salt and pepper to taste

DIRECTIONS

1. Bring a pot of water to a boil. Add the green beans and blanch for about 2-3 minutes until they're bright green and slightly tender. Drain and set aside.

2. In a large skillet or pan, heat the sesame oil over medium heat. Add minced garlic and grated ginger, sauté for about a minute until fragrant.

3. Add the blanched green beans to the skillet. Stir in soy sauce and honey, tossing the green beans to coat evenly. Cook for an additional 2-3 minutes until the green beans are crisp-tender.

4. Season with salt and pepper to taste. Sprinkle sesame seeds over the green beans, stir, and cook for another minute.

5. Remove from heat and serve your flavorful Sesame Ginger Green Beans. These Sesame Ginger Green Beans pair well with dishes like grilled chicken, stir-fried tofu, or as a side alongside a bowl of rice.

(per serving): Calories: 90 kcal, 10g, Proteins: 2g, Fats: 5g

Spiced Sweet Potato Wedges

2 servings | 35 minutes

INGREDIENTS

- 2 medium-sized sweet potatoes (500g or 1 lb)
- 30 ml (2 tablespoons) olive oil
- 5 gr (1 teaspoon) smoked paprika
- 2.5 g (1/2 teaspoon) ground cumin
- 2.5 g (1/2 teaspoon) garlic powder
- Salt and pepper to taste

DIRECTIONS

1. Preheat your oven to 425°F (220°C) and line a baking sheet with parchment paper.

2. Wash and scrub the sweet potatoes, then pat them dry. Leave the skin on for extra texture and nutrition. Cut the sweet potatoes into wedges, around 1.3 cm (1/2 inch) thick.

3. In a large bowl, toss the sweet potato wedges with olive oil, smoked paprika, ground cumin, garlic powder, salt, and pepper until evenly coated.

4. Spread the seasoned wedges in a single layer on the prepared baking sheet.

5. Bake for about 20-25 minutes, flipping halfway through, until the sweet potatoes are tender on the inside and crispy on the outside.

6. Once done, remove from the oven and let them cool slightly before serving. These Spiced Sweet Potato Wedges can be served as a hearty side dish alongside burgers, grilled chicken, or a simple salad for a complete and satisfying meal.

(per serving): Calories: 250 kcal, ...0 g, Proteins: 3 g, Fats: 9 g

Mexican Street Corn Salad

🍴 2 servings   🕐 20 minutes

INGREDIENTS

- 2 cups (approximately 300g) corn kernels (fresh, canned, or frozen and thawed)
- 2 tablespoons mayonnaise
- 2 tablespoons sour cream
- 1/4 cup (about 30g) cotija cheese or feta cheese, crumbled
- 1 tablespoon fresh cilantro, chopped
- 1/2 teaspoon chili powder (adjust to taste)
- 1/2 lime, juiced
- Salt and pepper to taste

DIRECTIONS

1. If using fresh corn, grill the corn on a stovetop grill or in a skillet until lightly charred. If using canned or thawed frozen corn, skip this step.

2. In a bowl, combine the corn kernels, mayonnaise, sour cream, crumbled cotija or feta cheese, chopped cilantro, chili powder, lime juice, salt, and pepper. Mix until all ingredients are evenly coated.

3. Taste and adjust seasoning if needed. Add more chili powder for extra heat or lime juice for tanginess.

4. Serve the Mexican Street Corn Salad chilled or at room temperature. It pairs wonderfully with grilled meats such as chicken, steak, or fish. It can also be served as a side dish alongside tacos, quesadillas, or as a topping for nachos.

(per serving): Calories: 210 kcal, Carbohydrates: 22g, Proteins: 5g, Fats: 13g

CHAPTER 5
SOUPS & STEWS SHOWDOWN

Hearty Beef Stew

🍴 2 servings   🕐 90 minutes

INGREDIENTS

- 450g (1 lb) beef chuck roast, cubed
- 2 tablespoons (30ml) olive oil
- 1 onion, chopped
- 2 cloves garlic, minced
- 2 large carrots, sliced
- 2 potatoes, diced
- 1 can (400g/14 oz) diced tomatoes
- 480ml (2 cups) beef broth
- 5ml (1 teaspoon) Worcestershire sauce
- 1 teaspoon dried thyme
- Salt and pepper to taste

DIRECTIONS

1. Heat 30ml olive oil in a large pot over medium-high heat. Brown the 450g beef cubes on all sides. Remove and set aside.

2. In the same pot, sauté the chopped onions and minced garlic until translucent.

3. Add the browned beef back into the pot along with carrots, potatoes, diced tomatoes (with their juices), beef broth, Worcestershire sauce, thyme, salt, and pepper. Bring to a boil.

4. Reduce heat to low, cover the pot, and simmer for about 1.5 hours or until the beef is tender and the vegetables are cooked through, stirring occasionally.

5. Adjust seasoning if needed and serve hot. This hearty Beef Stew can be served with crusty bread, dinner rolls, or over a bed of cooked rice or mashed potatoes for a complete and filling meal.

(per serving): Calories: 580 kcal, 2g, Proteins: 42g, Fats: 33g

Beef Chili

🍴 2 servings   🕐 40 minutes

INGREDIENTS

- 225g (8 oz) ground beef
- 1 small onion, diced
- 2 cloves garlic, minced
- 1 can (400g/14 oz) diced tomatoes
- 1 can (400g/14 oz) kidney beans, drained and rinsed
- 1 cup (250ml) beef broth
- 1 tablespoon chili powder
- 1 teaspoon cumin
- Salt and pepper to taste
- Optional toppings: shredded cheese, sour cream, chopped green onions

DIRECTIONS

1. In a pot or skillet over medium heat, cook the ground beef, breaking it apart with a spoon, until it's browned. Drain excess fat if needed.

2. Add diced onions and minced garlic to the beef. Sauté for 2-3 minutes until the onions are translucent.

3. Stir in diced tomatoes, kidney beans, beef broth, chili powder, cumin, salt, and pepper. Bring the mixture to a boil.

4. Reduce the heat to low, cover the pot, and let it simmer for about 20-25 minutes, stirring occasionally.

5. Taste and adjust seasoning if needed. This hearty Beef Chili can be served with a variety of sides such as cornbread, tortilla chips, rice, or even over baked potatoes for a filling meal. Adjust the spice level according to preference and serve with desired toppings like shredded cheese, sour cream, or chopped green onions, for extra flavor and satisfaction!

(per serving): Calories: 400 kcal, 8g, Proteins: 26g, Fats: 21g

Chicken Noodle Soup

🍴 2 servings   🕐 35 minutes

INGREDIENTS

- 2 boneless, skinless chicken breasts (225g / 8 oz), diced
- 1 tablespoon olive oil (15ml)
- 1 small onion, finely chopped
- 2 cloves garlic, minced
- 4 cups (1 liter) chicken broth
- 1 cup (250ml) water
- 1 medium carrot, sliced
- 1 celery stalk, chopped
- 1 cup (75g) egg noodles
- 1 bay leaf
- Salt and pepper to taste
- Fresh parsley for garnish (optional)

DIRECTIONS

1. In a pot, heat olive oil over medium heat. Add diced chicken and cook until browned, then remove from the pot and set aside.

2. In the same pot, sauté chopped onion and minced garlic until softened, about 2-3 minutes.

3. Pour in chicken broth and water. Add sliced carrot, chopped celery, bay leaf, salt, and pepper. Bring to a boil.

4. Reduce heat to a simmer. Add the cooked chicken back into the pot along with the egg noodles. Simmer for about 10-12 minutes or until noodles are tender and chicken is cooked through.

5. Remove the bay leaf. Taste and adjust seasoning if needed.

6. Serve hot, garnished with fresh parsley if desired. To make it even heartier, you can serve it with a side of crusty bread or a simple green salad.

(per serving): Calories: 300 kcal, 21g, Proteins: 32g, Fats: 9g

Lentil and Sausage Stew

🍴 2 servings   🕐 35 minutes

INGREDIENTS

- 1 tablespoon (15 ml) olive oil
- 200g (7 oz) smoked sausage, sliced
- 1 small onion, diced
- 2 cloves garlic, minced
- 1 cup (200g) dried lentils, rinsed and drained
- 4 cups (1 liter) chicken or vegetable broth
- 1 can (400g/14 oz) diced tomatoes
- 1 teaspoon paprika
- 1/2 teaspoon cumin
- Salt and pepper to taste
- Fresh parsley for garnish (optional)

DIRECTIONS

1. In a large pot or Dutch oven, heat olive oil over medium heat. Add the sliced sausage and cook until lightly browned, about 3-4 minutes.

2. Add diced onions and minced garlic, sautéing until onions are soft and fragrant, for about 3 minutes.

3. Stir in the rinsed lentils, chicken or vegetable broth, diced tomatoes (with their juices), paprika, cumin, salt, and pepper. Bring the mixture to a boil.

4. Reduce the heat to a simmer, cover the pot, and let it cook for about 20-25 minutes or until the lentils are tender, stirring occasionally.

5. Once the lentils are cooked through and the stew has thickened, taste and adjust seasoning if needed.

6. Serve hot, garnished with fresh parsley if desired. This hearty Lentil and Sausage Stew is quite filling and substantial, perfect as a standalone meal. To make it even heartier, serve it with a side of crusty bread or a simple green salad.

(per serving): Calories: 450 kcal, 0g, Proteins: 25g, Fats: 20g

Vegetable Minestrone Soup

🍴 2 servings 🕒 35 minutes

INGREDIENTS

- 2 tablespoons (15 ml) olive oil
- 1 small onion, diced
- 2 cloves garlic, minced
- 1 medium carrot, diced
- 1 celery stalk, diced
- 1 small zucchini, diced
- 1 can (400g/14 oz) diced tomatoes
- 4 cups (1 liter) vegetable broth
- 1/2 cup (75g) elbow macaroni or any small pasta
- 1 teaspoon dried basil
- 1 teaspoon dried oregano
- Salt and pepper to taste
- Grated Parmesan cheese (optional, for serving)

DIRECTIONS

1. In a large pot over medium heat, heat the olive oil. Add diced onions and minced garlic, sauté for 2-3 minutes until fragrant.

2. Add diced carrots, celery, and zucchini to the pot. Sauté for another 5 minutes until vegetables are slightly softened.

3. Pour in the diced tomatoes, vegetable broth, dried basil, dried oregano, salt, and pepper. Stir well and bring the mixture to a boil.

4. Once boiling, add the elbow macaroni or small pasta. Reduce heat to a simmer, cover the pot, and cook for about 12-15 minutes or until the pasta is cooked through and vegetables are tender.

5. Taste and adjust seasoning if needed. Serve the Vegetable Minestrone Soup hot, optionally topped with grated Parmesan cheese. This filling soup can be served with a side of crusty bread or a simple green salad for a complete and satisfying meal.

(per serving): Calories: 260 kcal, 38g, Proteins: 6g, Fats: 10g

MY WEEKLY MEAL PLANNER

Monday

Tuesday

Wednesday

Thursday

Friday

Saturday

Sunday

CHAPTER 6
SALAD SENSATIONS

Grilled Chicken Caesar Salad

🍴 2 servings ⏱ 30 minutes

INGREDIENTS

- 2 boneless, skinless chicken breasts (approx. 350g/12 oz)
- 1 tablespoon olive oil
- Salt and black pepper to taste
- 1 head romaine lettuce, chopped
- 1/2 cup (60g) croutons
- 1/4 cup (25g) grated Parmesan cheese

Caesar Dressing:
- 1/4 cup (60ml) mayonnaise
- 2 tablespoons (30ml) lemon juice
- 1 teaspoon Dijon mustard
- 1 clove garlic, minced
- 1/4 cup (25g) grated Parmesan cheese
- Salt and black pepper to taste

DIRECTIONS

1. Preheat the grill or grill pan over medium-high heat. Rub chicken breasts with olive oil, season with salt and black pepper.

2. Grill the chicken for about 6-7 minutes per side or until the internal temperature reaches 165°F (75°C). Remove from heat and let it rest for a few minutes before slicing.

3. In a small bowl, whisk together the mayonnaise, lemon juice, Dijon mustard, minced garlic, grated Parmesan cheese, salt, and black pepper to make the Caesar dressing.

4. In a large bowl, toss the chopped romaine lettuce with half of the prepared Caesar dressing until well coated.

5. Divide the dressed lettuce onto serving plates, top with sliced grilled chicken, croutons, and additional grated Parmesan cheese. Drizzle the remaining Caesar dressing over the chicken. This Grilled Chicken Caesar Salad can be served as a standalone meal or paired with a slice of garlic bread.

(per serving): Calories: 380 kcal, ...g, Proteins: 40g, Fats: 20g

Tex-Mex Beef Salad

🍴 2 servings   🕒 25 minutes

INGREDIENTS

- 250g (9 oz) lean ground beef
- 1 tablespoon olive oil
- 1 teaspoon chili powder
- 1 teaspoon cumin
- Salt and pepper to taste
- 4 cups (120g) mixed salad greens (lettuce, spinach, etc.)
- 1/2 cup (75g) canned black beans, drained and rinsed
- 1/2 cup (60g) corn kernels (canned or frozen, thawed)
- 1 avocado, diced
- 1/2 cup (60g) cherry tomatoes, halved
- 1/4 cup (30g) shredded cheddar cheese
- 1/4 cup (60ml) salsa
- 2 tablespoons sour cream (optional, for serving)

DIRECTIONS

1. Heat olive oil in a skillet over medium heat. Add the ground beef and cook until browned, breaking it apart with a spatula as it cooks, about 5-6 minutes.

2. Season the beef with chili powder, cumin, salt, and pepper. Stir well to combine and cook for an additional 2-3 minutes. Remove from heat and let it cool slightly.

3. In a large mixing bowl, combine the mixed salad greens, black beans, corn, diced avocado, cherry tomatoes, and shredded cheddar cheese.

4. Divide the salad mixture between two plates or bowls. Top each serving with the cooked seasoned beef.

Drizzle each serving with salsa and, if desired, a dollop of sour cream. This Tex-Mex Beef Salad can be served with a side of tortilla chips or warm tortillas for a complete and filling Tex-Mex meal.

(per serving): Calories: 480 kcal, 5g, Proteins: 26g, Fats: 32g

Greek Chickpea Salad

🍴 2 servings   🕐 10 minutes

INGREDIENTS

- 1 can (400g/14 oz) chickpeas, drained and rinsed
- 1 medium cucumber, diced
- 1 cup (150g) cherry tomatoes, halved
- 1/2 red onion, thinly sliced
- 1/2 cup (75g) Kalamata olives, pitted and halved
- 2 tablespoons chopped fresh parsley
- 1/2 cup (75g) crumbled feta cheese
- 2 tablespoons extra virgin olive oil
- 1 tablespoon red wine vinegar
- 1/2 teaspoon dried oregano
- Salt and pepper to taste

DIRECTIONS

1. In a mixing bowl, combine the chickpeas, diced cucumber, cherry tomatoes, sliced red onion, Kalamata olives, chopped parsley, and crumbled feta cheese.

2. In a small bowl, whisk together the extra virgin olive oil, red wine vinegar, dried oregano, salt, and pepper to create the dressing.

3. Pour the dressing over the salad ingredients in the mixing bowl and toss gently to coat everything evenly.

4. Taste and adjust seasoning if needed. Allow the flavors to meld together for a few minutes before serving. This Greek Chickpea Salad can be served as a satisfying standalone meal or as a side dish alongside grilled chicken, fish, or lamb. Alternatively, pair it with toasted pita bread or hummus for a complete and filling meal.

(per serving): Calories: 320 kcal, 0g, Proteins: 10g, Fats: 18g

Loaded Cobb Salad

🍽 2 servings 🕐 15 minutes

INGREDIENTS

- 2 cups (150g) mixed salad greens
- 2 hard-boiled eggs, sliced
- 6 slices cooked bacon, chopped
- 1 grilled chicken breast, diced
- 1 avocado, diced
- 1 cup (150g) cherry tomatoes, halved
- 1/2 cup (75g) crumbled blue cheese or feta cheese
- 2 tablespoons chopped chives or green onions
- Ranch or blue cheese dressing (optional)

DIRECTIONS

1. Arrange the mixed salad greens in a large serving bowl or plate as the base of the salad.

2. Arrange sliced hard-boiled eggs, chopped bacon, diced grilled chicken breast, diced avocado, halved cherry tomatoes, crumbled blue cheese, and chopped chives in rows on top of the greens.

3. Drizzle with your choice of dressing (Ranch or blue cheese dressing works well with this salad), or serve the dressing on the side. This Loaded Cobb Salad is substantial on its own but can be served with a side of crusty bread or garlic bread for a more filling meal.

(per serving): Calories: 520 kcal, 2g, Proteins: 32g, Fats: 39g

Asian Sesame Steak Salad

2 servings | **25 minutes**

INGREDIENTS

- 300g (10 oz) sirloin steak
- 6 cups mixed greens (lettuce, spinach, arugula, etc.)
- 1/2 cup (75g) sliced bell peppers (any color)
- 1/2 cup (75g) sliced cucumber
- 1/4 cup (40g) shredded carrots
- 2 tablespoons chopped green onions
- 2 tablespoons sesame seeds

For the Marinade:
- 2 tablespoons (30 ml) soy sauce
- 2 tablespoons (30 ml) sesame oil
- 1 tablespoon rice vinegar
- 1 tablespoon honey
- 2 cloves garlic, minced
- 1 teaspoon grated ginger
- Salt and pepper to taste

For the Dressing:
- 2 tablespoons (30 ml) soy sauce
- 1 tablespoon (15 ml) sesame oil
- 1 tablespoon rice vinegar
- 1 teaspoon honey
- 1 teaspoon grated ginger
- 1 clove garlic, minced

DIRECTIONS

1. In a bowl, mix together all the ingredients for the marinade. Place the steak in a ziplock bag or shallow dish, pour the marinade over it, and let it marinate for at least 30 minutes in the refrigerator.

2. Heat a grill pan or skillet over medium-high heat. Remove the steak from the marinade and discard the excess marinade. Cook the steak for about 3-4 minutes per side for medium-rare (adjust according to desired doneness). Once cooked, let it rest for a few minutes before slicing thinly.

3. In a large bowl, toss together the mixed greens, sliced bell peppers, sliced cucumber, shredded carrots, green onions, and sesame seeds.

4. In a small bowl, whisk together the ingredients for the dressing.

5. Divide the salad mixture between two plates, top each with sliced steak, and drizzle the dressing over the salad. This Asian Sesame Steak Salad can be served with a side of steamed rice or garlic noodles for a more substantial meal.

(per serving): Calories: 370 kcal, 5g, Proteins: 27g, Fats: 23g

MY WEEKLY MEAL PLANNER

Monday	Tuesday
Wednesday	Thursday
Friday	Saturday
Sunday	

CHAPTER 7
SNACK ATTACK EXTRAVAGANZA

Garlic Parmesan Chicken Wings and Carrot Sticks

🍴 2 servings   🕐 50 minutes

INGREDIENTS

- 12 chicken wings, split into wingettes and drumettes (about 700g)
- 2 tablespoons (30 ml) olive oil
- 3 cloves garlic, minced
- 1/3 cup (40g) grated Parmesan cheese
- 1 teaspoon dried parsley
- 4 large carrots, peeled and cut into sticks
- Salt and pepper to taste
- Cooking spray (optional)

DIRECTIONS

1. Preheat your oven to 400°F (200°C). Line a baking sheet with parchment paper or foil for easy cleanup. Alternatively, you can use a wire rack on top of the baking sheet.

2. In a large mixing bowl, toss the chicken wings with olive oil, minced garlic, grated Parmesan cheese, dried parsley, salt, and pepper until evenly coated.

3. Arrange the seasoned chicken wings on the prepared baking sheet in a single layer. If using a wire rack, place the rack on the baking sheet and arrange the wings on it.

4. Place the carrot sticks on another baking sheet or beside the chicken wings on the same sheet.

5. Bake the chicken wings in the preheated oven for 35-40 minutes or until they are golden brown and crispy, flipping them halfway through the cooking time for even crispiness. Roast the carrots for 20-25 minutes or until tender but slightly crisp.

6. Optional: If you prefer extra crispy wings, broil them for an additional 2-3 minutes at the end of the cooking time.

7. Serve the Garlic Parmesan Chicken Wings and carrot sticks hot, garnished with additional grated Parmesan cheese and chopped parsley if desired.

(per serving): Calories: 540 kcal, 4g, Proteins: 40g, Fats: 35g

Homemade Pizza Rolls

🍴 2 servings 🕐 25 minutes
4 pizza rolls per serving

INGREDIENTS

- 1 sheet of puff pastry (thawed)
- 1/2 cup (120ml) pizza sauce or marinara sauce
- 1 cup (115g) shredded mozzarella cheese
- 16 slices pepperoni or your choice of toppings
- 1 egg (for egg wash)
- Italian seasoning or dried oregano (optional)
- Grated Parmesan cheese (optional, for sprinkling)

DIRECTIONS

1. Preheat the oven to 400°F (200°C) and line a baking sheet with parchment paper.

2. On a lightly floured surface, unfold the thawed puff pastry sheet. Cut it into 8 equal squares.

3. Spoon a small amount (about 1 tablespoon) of pizza sauce onto each pastry square, spreading it slightly. Leave a border around the edges.

4. Place 2 slices of pepperoni on top of the sauce on each square and sprinkle shredded mozzarella cheese over the pepperoni.

5. Roll up each square into a tight spiral, starting from one end and rolling towards the other end. Repeat for all squares.

6. Place the rolls seam-side down on the prepared baking sheet. Beat the egg in a small bowl and brush the tops of the rolls with the egg wash. Optionally, sprinkle Italian seasoning or dried oregano and grated Parmesan cheese on top.

7. Bake for about 12-15 minutes or until the rolls are golden brown and puffed up.

8. Serve the Homemade Pizza Rolls hot and enjoy! These Pizza Rolls can be served with a side of additional marinara sauce or ranch dressing for dipping, along with a side salad or veggies for a complete snack or light meal.

(per serving): Calories: 450 kcal, ...0g, Proteins: 13g, Fats: 30g

Buffalo Chicken Dip with Tortilla Chips

2 servings | 30 minutes

INGREDIENTS

- 1 cup (150g) cooked chicken, shredded or diced
- 1/2 cup (120ml) buffalo sauce
- 1/2 cup (120g) cream cheese, softened
- 1/4 cup (60ml) ranch or blue cheese dressing
- 1/4 cup (30g) shredded cheddar cheese
- Tortilla chips for serving

DIRECTIONS

1. Preheat the oven to 350°F (175°C).

2. In a mixing bowl, combine the cooked chicken, buffalo sauce, softened cream cheese, and ranch or blue cheese dressing. Mix well until thoroughly combined.

3. Spread the mixture evenly into an oven-safe dish and sprinkle the shredded cheddar cheese on top.

4. Bake in the preheated oven for about 15-20 minutes or until the dip is bubbly and the cheese is melted and lightly golden on top.

5. Remove from the oven and let it cool for a few minutes.

6. Serve the Buffalo Chicken Dip hot with tortilla chips for dipping. This hearty and filling Buffalo Chicken Dip is perfect for serving with tortilla chips, carrot sticks, celery, or sliced bell peppers for a flavorful and satisfying snack.

(per serving): Calories: 380 kcal, 8g, Proteins: 18g, Fats: 32g

BBQ Pulled Pork Sliders

🍴 2 servings   🕒 180 min

INGREDIENTS

- 500g (1 lb) pork shoulder or pork butt
- 1 cup (250ml) BBQ sauce (plus extra for serving)
- 1/2 cup (120ml) chicken or vegetable broth
- 1 tablespoon brown sugar
- 1 teaspoon garlic powder
- 1 teaspoon onion powder
- Salt and pepper to taste
- 4 slider buns or small dinner rolls
- Coleslaw or sliced pickles (optional, for serving)

DIRECTIONS

1. Preheat your oven to 325°F (165°C).

2. Place the pork shoulder in a baking dish. In a bowl, mix together BBQ sauce, chicken broth, brown sugar, garlic powder, onion powder, salt, and pepper. Pour this mixture over the pork, ensuring it's well coated.

3. Cover the baking dish with foil and roast in the preheated oven for 2.5 - 3 hours or until the pork is tender and easily pulls apart with a fork.

4. Remove the pork from the oven and shred it using two forks. Mix in additional BBQ sauce if desired for extra flavor and moisture.

5. To assemble sliders, pile the pulled pork onto slider buns or dinner rolls. Top with coleslaw or sliced pickles if using. These BBQ Pulled Pork Sliders pair well with a side of crispy potato wedges or a simple green salad.

(per serving): Calories: 540 kcal, 4g, Proteins: 39g, Fats: 16g

Crispy Fried Pickles

🍴 2 servings 🕐 20 minutes

INGREDIENTS

- 1 cup (150g) dill pickle slices, drained and patted dry
- 1/2 cup (60g) all-purpose flour
- 1/2 teaspoon garlic powder
- 1/2 teaspoon paprika
- 1/4 teaspoon cayenne pepper (optional)
- 1/2 cup (120ml) buttermilk
- 1 cup (100g) breadcrumbs (or panko breadcrumbs)
- Oil for frying (enough to cover the bottom of the pan)

DIRECTIONS

1. In a shallow bowl, mix together the flour, garlic powder, paprika, and cayenne pepper (if using).

2. In another bowl, pour the buttermilk.

3. Dip each pickle slice into the flour mixture, then into the buttermilk, and finally into the breadcrumbs, pressing gently to coat.

4. In a skillet or frying pan, heat oil over medium-high heat. Once hot, add the coated pickle slices in batches, frying for about 2-3 minutes per side or until golden brown and crispy. Remove and place on a paper towel-lined plate to drain excess oil.

5. Repeat the frying process with the remaining pickle slices.

6. Serve the Crispy Fried Pickles hot and crispy! They can be served with a side of ranch dressing, sriracha mayo, or your favorite tangy dipping sauce.

(per serving): Calories: 230 kcal, 38g, Proteins: 6g, Fats: 5g

MY WEEKLY MEAL PLANNER

Monday

Tuesday

Wednesday

Thursday

Friday

Saturday

Sunday

CHAPTER 8
DECADENT DESSERT DELIGHTS

Heavenly Berry Parfait

2 servings | 10 minutes

INGREDIENTS

- 1 cup (240g) Greek yogurt
- 1 cup (150g) mixed berries (strawberries, blueberries, raspberries)
- 2 tablespoons honey or maple syrup
- 1/2 cup (60g) granola or crushed nuts (optional)
- Fresh mint leaves for garnish (optional)

DIRECTIONS

1. In two serving glasses or jars, start layering the parfait. Begin with a spoonful of Greek yogurt at the bottom of each glass.

2. Add a layer of mixed berries on top of the yogurt in each glass. Drizzle a tablespoon of honey or maple syrup over the berries.

3. Repeat the layers—yogurt, berries, sweetener—until the glasses are filled, ending with a layer of berries on top.

4. Optionally, sprinkle granola or crushed nuts over the final berry layer for added crunch and texture.

5. Garnish with fresh mint leaves if desired. It's delicious on its own but can also be served with a drizzle of chocolate sauce or a dollop of whipped cream for an extra indulgence.

(per serving): Calories: 200 kcal, 0g, Proteins: 12g, Fats: 3g

Chocolate Chip Cookie Skillet

🍴 2 servings 🕒 25 minutes

INGREDIENTS

- 4 tablespoons (60g) unsalted butter, melted
- 1/4 cup (50g) granulated sugar
- 1/4 cup (50g) packed brown sugar
- 1/2 teaspoon vanilla extract
- 1 large egg
- 3/4 cup (95g) all-purpose flour
- 1/2 teaspoon baking soda
- 1/4 teaspoon salt
- 1/2 cup (90g) chocolate chips
- Vanilla ice cream (optional, for serving)

DIRECTIONS

1. Preheat your oven to 350°F (175°C). Grease a small oven-safe skillet or baking dish.

2. In a mixing bowl, whisk together the melted butter, granulated sugar, brown sugar, and vanilla extract until well combined.

3. Add the egg to the mixture and whisk until smooth.

4. Stir in the flour, baking soda, and salt until just combined. Fold in the chocolate chips.

5. Transfer the cookie dough into the greased skillet, spreading it evenly.

6. Bake in the preheated oven for about 12-15 minutes or until the edges are golden brown and the center is slightly set.

7. Remove from the oven and let it cool for a few minutes. Optionally, serve the Chocolate Chip Cookie Skillet warm with a scoop of vanilla ice cream on top.

Nutritional Info (per serving): Calories: Approximately 480 kcal, Carbohydrates: 65g, Proteins: 6g, Fats: 25g

Caramel Pretzel Chocolate Bark

2 servings | 70 minutes

INGREDIENTS

- 200g (7 oz) dark or milk chocolate, chopped
- 1/2 cup (60g) mini pretzels, broken into pieces
- 1/4 cup (50g) caramel sauce (store-bought or homemade)
- Sea salt flakes (optional, for topping)

DIRECTIONS

1. Line a baking sheet with parchment paper.

2. Melt the chopped chocolate using a double boiler or microwave, stirring occasionally until smooth.

3. Pour the melted chocolate onto the prepared baking sheet and spread it evenly to about 1/4 inch thickness.

4. Drizzle the caramel sauce over the melted chocolate and use a toothpick or knife to create swirls.

5. Sprinkle the broken pretzel pieces evenly over the chocolate-caramel mixture, gently pressing them in.

6. If desired, lightly sprinkle sea salt flakes over the top for a sweet and salty contrast.

7. Place the baking sheet in the refrigerator for at least 1 hour or until the bark is completely set.

8. Once set, break the bark into pieces using your hands or a knife. This Caramel Pretzel Chocolate Bark can be served as a delicious dessert on its own or paired with a scoop of vanilla ice cream for an extra indulgent treat.

(per serving): Calories: 350 kcal, 45g, Proteins: 4g, Fats: 18g

Churro Bites

🍴 2 servings   🕐 25 minutes

INGREDIENTS

- 1/2 cup (120ml) water
- 2 tablespoons (28g) unsalted butter
- 2 tablespoons (25g) granulated sugar
- 1/2 teaspoon vanilla extract
- 1/2 cup (60g) all-purpose flour
- 1/4 cup (50g) granulated sugar (for coating)
- 1 teaspoon ground cinnamon

DIRECTIONS

1. In a saucepan, combine water, butter, and sugar. Bring to a boil, then remove from heat. Stir in the vanilla extract.

2. Add the flour to the mixture and stir until it forms a dough-like consistency and pulls away from the sides of the pan.

3. Transfer the dough to a piping bag fitted with a star tip (or a plastic bag with the corner snipped off).

4. Heat oil in a deep skillet or pot over medium heat. Pipe small portions of the dough directly into the hot oil, cutting it with scissors. Fry until golden brown (about 2-3 minutes per batch), then remove with a slotted spoon and drain on paper towels.

5. In a separate bowl, mix sugar and ground cinnamon. Roll the fried churro bites in the cinnamon-sugar mixture while they're still warm.

6. Serve the Churro Bites warm and crispy. Churro Bites are delightful on their own, but they can be served with a side of chocolate or caramel sauce for dipping to enhance the sweetness. They are also great with a scoop of vanilla ice cream.

(per serving): Calories: 250 kcal, 30g, Proteins: 2g, Fats: 14g

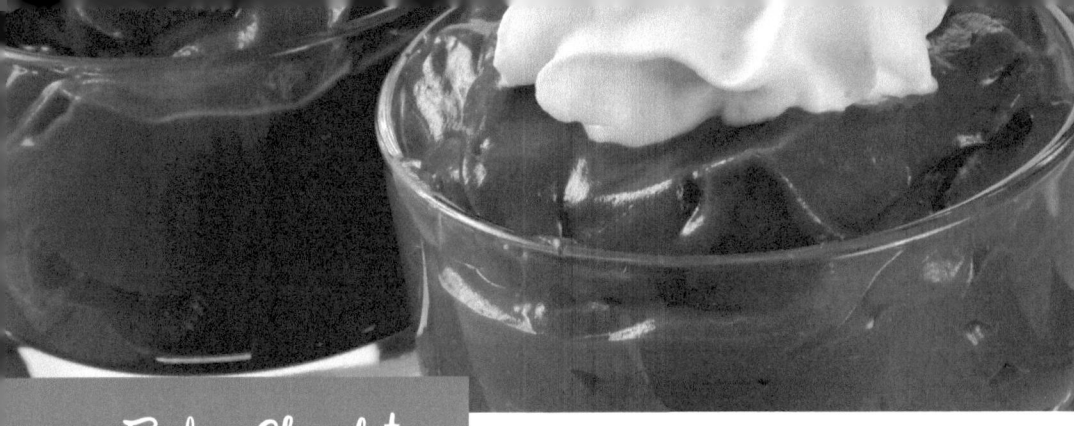

Fudgy Chocolate Pudding

🍴 2 servings   🕐 75 minutes

INGREDIENTS

- 3 tablespoons granulated sugar (45g)
- 2 tablespoons unsweetened cocoa powder (14g)
- 2 tablespoons cornstarch (16g)
- Pinch of salt
- 1 1/2 cups whole milk (375ml)
- 1/2 teaspoon vanilla extract (2.5ml)
- 50g dark chocolate, chopped (about 2 oz)
- Whipped cream or chocolate shavings (optional, for serving)

DIRECTIONS

1. In a saucepan, whisk together 3 tablespoons granulated sugar, 2 tablespoons unsweetened cocoa powder, 2 tablespoons cornstarch, and a pinch of salt until well combined.

2. Gradually pour in 1 1/2 cups whole milk while whisking continuously to avoid lumps.

3. Place the saucepan over medium heat, stirring constantly until the mixture thickens and comes to a gentle boil, about 5-7 minutes.

4. Remove the saucepan from heat and stir in 1/2 teaspoon vanilla extract and 50g chopped dark chocolate until the chocolate is melted and the mixture is smooth.

5. Pour the pudding into serving bowls or cups. Cover with plastic wrap directly touching the surface to prevent a skin from forming. Refrigerate for 1-2 hours until chilled and set.

6. Serve the Fudgy Chocolate Pudding cold, optionally topped with whipped cream or chocolate shavings for added flair.

(per serving): Calories: 250 kcal, Carbohydrates: 35g, Proteins: 6g, Fats: 11g

MY WEEKLY MEAL PLANNER

Monday

Tuesday

Wednesday

Thursday

Friday

Saturday

Sunday

CHAPTER 9
FISH & SEAFOOD FIESTA

Grilled Lemon Garlic Shrimp

2 servings | 15 minutes

INGREDIENTS

- 300g (10 oz) large shrimp, peeled and deveined
- 2 tablespoons (30 ml) olive oil
- 2 cloves garlic, minced
- Zest and juice of 1 lemon
- 1 tablespoon chopped fresh parsley
- Salt and pepper to taste
- Skewers (if using wooden skewers, soak them in water for 30 minutes)

DIRECTIONS

1. Preheat the grill to medium-high heat.

2. In a bowl, mix together olive oil, minced garlic, lemon zest, lemon juice, chopped parsley, salt, and pepper.

3. Add the cleaned shrimp to the bowl and toss to coat evenly with the marinade. Let it marinate for about 5-10 minutes.

4. Thread the marinated shrimp onto skewers.

5. Place the shrimp skewers on the preheated grill and cook for 2-3 minutes on each side, or until shrimp are pink and opaque.

6. Remove the shrimp skewers from the grill and serve hot. These Grilled Lemon Garlic Shrimp can be served with a side of steamed rice, quinoa, or a fresh salad to create a complete meal. Consider adding a side of grilled vegetables or a lemon wedge for an extra burst of flavor.

(per serving): Calories: 210 kcal, ...g, Proteins: 24g, Fats: 11g

Cajun Blackened Salmon

2 servings | **20 minutes**

INGREDIENTS

- 2 salmon fillets (about 170-225g each, 6-8 oz)
- 30ml (2 tbsp) olive oil
- 15ml (1 tbsp) Cajun seasoning
- 2.5ml (1/2 tsp) paprika
- 2.5ml (1/2 tsp) garlic powder
- 2.5ml (1/2 tsp) onion powder
- 2.5ml (1/2 tsp) dried thyme
- 2.5ml (1/2 tsp) dried oregano
- Salt and pepper to taste
- Lemon wedges for serving (optional)

DIRECTIONS

1. In a small bowl, mix together Cajun seasoning, paprika, garlic powder, onion powder, dried thyme, dried oregano, salt, and pepper.

2. Rub the salmon fillets evenly with olive oil, then generously coat both sides with the Cajun seasoning mixture.

3. Heat a skillet or frying pan over medium-high heat. Once hot, add a splash of olive oil to prevent sticking.

4. Place the seasoned salmon fillets in the pan, skin-side down if applicable. Cook for about 3-4 minutes per side, or until the salmon is cooked through and has a blackened crust on the outside.

5. Remove the salmon from the pan and let it rest for a minute.

6. Serve the Cajun Blackened Salmon hot, optionally with lemon wedges for a citrusy kick. It can also be served with a side of steamed vegetables, a simple green salad, or rice to make a complete and filling meal.

(per serving): Calories: 350 kcal, Proteins: 34g, Fats: 23g

Salmon Burgers

🍴 2 servings   🕐 20 minutes

INGREDIENTS

- 400g (14 oz) skinless salmon fillet, chopped into small pieces
- 1/4 cup (25g) breadcrumbs
- 1 egg, lightly beaten
- 2 tablespoons chopped fresh dill (or 1 tablespoon dried dill)
- 2 tablespoons chopped green onions
- 1 tablespoon Dijon mustard
- 1 tablespoon lemon juice
- Salt and pepper to taste
- 2 hamburger buns
- Lettuce, tomato slices, and any desired toppings

DIRECTIONS

1. In a mixing bowl, combine chopped salmon, breadcrumbs, beaten egg, chopped dill, green onions, Dijon mustard, lemon juice, salt, and pepper. Mix until well combined.

2. Divide the mixture into two equal portions and shape each portion into a patty.

3. Heat a non-stick skillet or grill pan over medium heat. Lightly oil the surface.

4. Place the salmon patties onto the skillet or grill pan and cook for about 4-5 minutes on each side, or until cooked through and golden brown on the outside.

5. Toast the hamburger buns if desired. Place the cooked salmon patties on the buns, add lettuce, tomato slices, and any desired toppings.

6. Serve the Salmon Burgers hot and enjoy! They can be served with a side of sweet potato fries, coleslaw, or a simple mixed green salad for a complete and filling meal.

(per serving): Calories: 350 kcal, 1g, Proteins: 30g, Fats: 16g

Grilled Cajun Garlic Butter Lobster Tails

🍴 2 servings   🕐 20 minutes

INGREDIENTS

- 2 lobster tails (about 225-230g each)
- 4 tablespoons unsalted butter, melted (approximately 60g)
- 2 cloves garlic, minced
- 1 teaspoon Cajun seasoning
- 1 tablespoon fresh parsley, chopped
- Salt and pepper to taste
- Lemon wedges for serving

DIRECTIONS

1. Preheat the grill to medium-high heat.

2. Using kitchen shears, cut through the top of the lobster tails lengthwise, stopping at the tail. Gently spread the shell open to expose the meat.

3. In a small bowl, combine melted butter (approximately 60ml), minced garlic, Cajun seasoning, chopped parsley, salt, and pepper.

4. Brush the garlic butter mixture generously over the exposed lobster meat.

5. Place the lobster tails shell side down on the grill and cook for about 5-7 minutes, until the meat is opaque and slightly charred, brushing with the remaining garlic butter mixture while grilling.

6. Remove the lobster tails from the grill and serve hot with lemon wedges on the side. These Grilled Cajun Garlic Butter Lobster Tails pair wonderfully with a side of garlic butter roasted vegetables or a simple garden salad for a well-balanced meal.

(per serving): Calories: 280 kcal, 1g, Proteins: 28g, Fats: 18g

Spicy Sriracha Tuna Wraps

2 servings | 20 minutes

INGREDIENTS

- 2 cans (5 oz/140g each) tuna in water, drained
- 3 tablespoons mayonnaise
- 1 tablespoon Sriracha sauce (adjust for spice preference)
- 1 teaspoon lemon juice
- 1/4 cup (30g) diced celery
- 1/4 cup (30g) diced red bell pepper
- 2 large lettuce leaves or tortilla wraps
- Salt and pepper to taste

DIRECTIONS

1. In a mixing bowl, combine drained tuna, mayonnaise, Sriracha sauce, lemon juice, diced celery, and diced red bell pepper. Mix well until all ingredients are evenly combined.

2. Season the tuna mixture with salt and pepper to taste. Adjust Sriracha sauce for desired spice level.

3. Lay out the lettuce leaves or tortilla wraps. Divide the spicy tuna mixture evenly and spoon onto the center of each leaf or wrap.

4. Roll up the lettuce leaves or wraps tightly, enclosing the filling.

5. Serve the Spicy Sriracha Tuna Wraps immediately. It can be served with a side of sliced vegetables, such as carrots, cucumber, or cherry tomatoes, or paired with a side salad or some crispy potato chips for a complete meal.

(per serving): Calories: 250 kcal, Carbohydrates: 8g, Proteins: 30g, Fats: 13g

MY WEEKLY MEAL PLANNER

Monday	Tuesday

Wednesday	Thursday

Friday	Saturday

Sunday	

CHAPTER 10
POULTRY & BEEF PERFECTION

Korean BBQ Chicken Bowls

🍴 2 servings 🕐 30 minutes

INGREDIENTS

- 2 boneless, skinless chicken breasts, cut into bite-sized pieces (about 350g/12 oz)
- 2 tablespoons soy sauce
- 1 tablespoon honey
- 1 tablespoon sesame oil
- 2 cloves garlic, minced
- 1 teaspoon grated ginger
- 1 tablespoon vegetable oil
- 1 cup (185g) cooked rice (white or brown)
- 1 cup (150g) shredded cabbage or lettuce
- 1 carrot, julienned
- 2 green onions, chopped
- Sesame seeds and sliced green onions for garnish (optional)

DIRECTIONS

1. In a bowl, mix soy sauce, honey, sesame oil, minced garlic, and grated ginger. Add the chicken pieces to the marinade and let it sit for 10-15 minutes.

2. Heat vegetable oil in a skillet over medium-high heat. Add the marinated chicken and cook for about 5-7 minutes, stirring occasionally, until the chicken is cooked through and slightly caramelized.

3. While the chicken is cooking, prepare the bowls. Divide cooked rice between two bowls. Top each bowl with shredded cabbage or lettuce, julienned carrots, and chopped green onions.

4. Once the chicken is cooked, divide it between the bowls, placing it on top of the veggies and rice.

5. Garnish with sesame seeds and additional sliced green onions if desired. You can serve with a side of kimchi, steamed vegetables, or a fried egg on top for added flavor and protein.

(per serving): Calories: 430 kcal, 7g, Proteins: 34g, Fats: 15g

Mexican Chipotle Chicken Chili

2 servings | 35 minutes

INGREDIENTS

- 2 tablespoons olive oil
- 1 small onion, diced
- 2 cloves garlic, minced
- 300g (10 oz) boneless, skinless chicken breasts, diced
- 1 can (400g/14 oz) black beans, drained and rinsed
- 1 can (400g/14 oz) diced tomatoes
- 1 cup (250ml) chicken broth
- 1 chipotle pepper in adobo sauce, minced (adjust to taste)
- 1 teaspoon ground cumin
- 1 teaspoon chili powder
- Salt and pepper to taste
- Fresh cilantro for garnish (optional)

DIRECTIONS

1. In a large pot or skillet over medium heat, heat olive oil. Add diced onions and minced garlic, sauté until onions are translucent, about 3-4 minutes.

2. Add diced chicken to the pot and cook until no longer pink, about 5-7 minutes.

3. Stir in black beans, diced tomatoes, chicken broth, minced chipotle pepper, ground cumin, chili powder, salt, and pepper. Bring the mixture to a boil.

4. Reduce heat to a simmer, cover the pot, and let it cook for about 15-20 minutes, stirring occasionally, until the chili thickens and flavors meld.

5. Taste and adjust seasoning if needed. Serve the Mexican Chipotle Chicken Chili hot, garnished with fresh cilantro if desired. It can be served with a side of warm tortillas, rice, or a dollop of sour cream and shredded cheese for added richness and flavor.

(per serving): Calories: 360 kcal, 4g, Proteins: 32g, Fats: 10g

Braised Beef Ragu Pasta

2 servings | 2hrs 10 min

INGREDIENTS
- 300g (10 oz) beef chuck or stewing beef, diced into small cubes
- 1 tablespoon olive oil
- 1 small onion, finely chopped
- 2 cloves garlic, minced
- 1 can (400g/14 oz) crushed tomatoes
- 1 cup (250ml) beef broth
- 1 teaspoon dried oregano
- 1 teaspoon dried basil
- Salt and pepper to taste
- 200g (7 oz) pasta of your choice (such as spaghetti or tagliatelle)
- Grated Parmesan cheese (optional, for serving)
- Chopped fresh parsley (optional, for garnish)

DIRECTIONS

1. Heat olive oil in a large skillet or pot over medium-high heat. Add diced beef and brown it on all sides for about 5 minutes. Remove beef and set aside.

2. In the same skillet, add chopped onions and minced garlic. Sauté until onions are soft and translucent.

3. Return the browned beef to the skillet. Add crushed tomatoes, beef broth, dried oregano, dried basil, salt, and pepper. Stir well, bring to a boil, then reduce heat to low.

4. Cover and simmer on low heat for about 1.5 to 2 hours, stirring occasionally, until the beef is tender and the sauce thickens. Add a bit more broth or water if needed.

5. While the ragu is simmering, cook the pasta according to package instructions until al dente. Drain and set aside.

6. Serve the Braised Beef Ragu over cooked pasta. Optionally, top with grated Parmesan cheese and chopped fresh parsley for extra flavor.

(per serving): Calories: 550 kcal, 0g, Proteins: 35g, Fats: 20g

Turkey Enchilada Casserole

🍴 2 servings   🕐 40 minutes

INGREDIENTS

- 1 tablespoon olive oil
- 1/2 small onion, diced
- 1/2 pound (225g) ground turkey
- 1 can (10 oz/300g) enchilada sauce
- 4 corn tortillas
- 1 cup (115g) shredded cheddar cheese
- 1/2 cup (120ml) sour cream
- Salt and pepper to taste
- Chopped fresh cilantro and sliced jalapeños for garnish (optional)

DIRECTIONS

1. Preheat your oven to 375°F (190°C).

2. In a skillet over medium heat, heat olive oil. Add diced onions and sauté until softened, then add ground turkey. Cook until turkey is browned, breaking it into smaller pieces with a spoon.

3. Stir in half of the enchilada sauce into the turkey mixture, let it simmer for a few minutes, then remove from heat.

4. In a baking dish, spread a thin layer of enchilada sauce on the bottom. Place two corn tortillas to cover the bottom of the dish, overlapping if necessary.

5. Spoon half of the turkey mixture over the tortillas, then sprinkle half of the shredded cheddar cheese on top.

6. Repeat the layers - place the remaining tortillas, turkey mixture, and finish with the rest of the shredded cheese.

7. Bake in the preheated oven for about 20-25 minutes until the cheese is bubbly and golden.

8. Serve the Turkey Enchilada Casserole hot, garnished with sour cream, cilantro, and sliced jalapeños if desired.

(per serving): Calories: 570 kcal, 3g, Proteins: 32g, Fats: 35g

Moroccan Spiced Beef Tagine

🍴 2 servings   🕐 50 minutes

INGREDIENTS

- 300g (10.5 oz) beef stew meat, cut into cubes
- 2 tablespoons olive oil
- 1 onion, finely chopped
- 2 cloves garlic, minced
- 1 teaspoon ground cumin
- 1 teaspoon ground coriander
- 1/2 teaspoon ground cinnamon
- 1/2 teaspoon ground ginger
- 1/2 teaspoon paprika
- 1/4 teaspoon cayenne pepper (adjust to taste)
- 1 can (400g/14 oz) diced tomatoes
- 1 cup (250ml) beef broth
- 1 cup (150g) carrots, sliced
- 1 cup (150g) potatoes, diced
- Salt and pepper to taste
- Fresh cilantro or parsley for garnish

DIRECTIONS

1. Heat olive oil in a large pot or Dutch oven over medium heat. Add the chopped onion and minced garlic, sauté for 2-3 minutes until fragrant.

2. Add the beef cubes to the pot and brown them on all sides for about 5-6 minutes.

3. Stir in the ground cumin, ground coriander, ground cinnamon, ground ginger, paprika, and cayenne pepper. Cook for another minute to toast the spices.

4. Pour in the diced tomatoes and beef broth. Bring the mixture to a simmer.

5. Add sliced carrots and diced potatoes to the pot. Season with salt and pepper. Cover and let it simmer for about 30 minutes or until the beef is tender and the vegetables are cooked through.

6. Taste and adjust seasoning if needed. Serve the Moroccan Spiced Beef Tagine hot, garnished with fresh cilantro or parsley. This filling dish can be served with couscous, rice, or crusty bread to soak up the flavorful sauce.

(per serving): Calories: 450 kcal, 5g, Proteins: 28g, Fats: 28g

MY WEEKLY MEAL PLANNER

Monday

Tuesday

Wednesday

Thursday

Friday

Saturday

Sunday

CHAPTER 11
DUCK, LAMB, & PORK PALOOZA

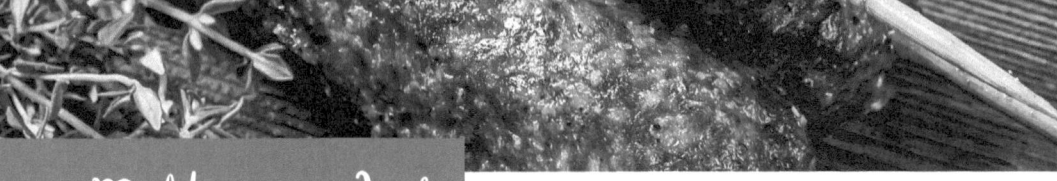

Mediterranean Lamb Kofta

2 servings | 30 minutes

INGREDIENTS

- 250g (9 oz) ground lamb
- 1 small onion, grated
- 2 cloves garlic, minced
- 1/4 cup (15g) fresh parsley, finely chopped
- 1 teaspoon ground cumin
- 1 teaspoon ground coriander
- 1/2 teaspoon paprika
- Salt and pepper to taste
- Olive oil for cooking

DIRECTIONS

1. In a mixing bowl, combine the ground lamb, grated onion, minced garlic, chopped parsley, ground cumin, ground coriander, paprika, salt, and pepper. Mix thoroughly until well combined.

2. Divide the lamb mixture into equal portions and shape each portion into sausage-shaped kofta or kebab sticks.

3. Heat a drizzle of olive oil in a skillet or grill pan over medium heat. Cook the lamb kofta for about 6-8 minutes, turning occasionally, until browned and cooked through.

4. Once cooked, transfer the lamb kofta to a plate lined with paper towels to absorb excess oil. Serve the Mediterranean Lamb Kofta with a side of fluffy rice, couscous, or pita bread. It pairs perfectly with a refreshing salad of chopped tomatoes, cucumbers, red onions, and a drizzle of yogurt sauce or tzatziki.

(per serving): Calories: 320 kcal, Proteins: 20g, Fats: 26g

Cuban Mojo Pork

🍴 2 servings   🕐 2hrs 10 min

INGREDIENTS

- 1 lb (450g) pork shoulder or pork loin, cut into chunks
- 4 cloves garlic, minced
- 1/4 cup (60ml) fresh orange juice
- 1/4 cup (60ml) fresh lime juice
- Zest of 1 lime
- 2 tablespoons (30ml) olive oil
- 1 teaspoon dried oregano
- 1 teaspoon cumin powder
- Salt and pepper to taste

DIRECTIONS

1. In a bowl, combine minced garlic, fresh orange juice, fresh lime juice, lime zest, olive oil, dried oregano, cumin powder, salt, and pepper. Mix well to create the marinade.

2. Place the pork chunks in a resealable plastic bag or a bowl. Pour the marinade over the pork, ensuring it's well-coated. Marinate in the refrigerator for at least 2 hours or overnight for better flavor.

3. Preheat the oven to 325°F (165°C). Transfer the marinated pork and marinade to an oven-safe dish or roasting pan.

4. Cover the dish with aluminum foil and bake for about 2 hours or until the pork is tender and easily shreddable. Check halfway through and baste the pork with the juices.

5. Once cooked, shred the pork using two forks. Serve the Cuban Mojo Pork hot. This Cuban Mojo Pork can be served with rice, black beans, or as a filling for tacos or burritos.

(per serving): Calories: 380 kcal, Proteins: 35g, Fats: 22g

Duck Breast with Cherry Port Sauce

🍴 2 servings   🕐 30 minutes

INGREDIENTS

- 2 duck breasts (about 400g/14 oz total), skin scored
- Salt and pepper to taste
- 1 tablespoon olive oil
- 1/2 cup (120ml) port wine
- 1/4 cup (60ml) chicken or beef broth
- 1/4 cup (60ml) cherry jam or preserves
- 1 tablespoon balsamic vinegar
- 1 tablespoon unsalted butter

DIRECTIONS

1. Pat dry the duck breasts with paper towels and season both sides generously with salt and pepper.

2. Heat a skillet over medium-high heat and add olive oil. Place the duck breasts in the skillet, skin side down, and cook for about 6-8 minutes until the skin is crispy and golden brown. Flip and cook for an additional 3-4 minutes for medium-rare or until desired doneness. Remove the duck breasts and let them rest on a cutting board.

3. In the same skillet, pour in the port wine and chicken or beef broth. Stir and scrape up any browned bits from the bottom of the pan. Add cherry jam and balsamic vinegar, stirring until the sauce thickens slightly.

4. Reduce the heat to low and whisk in the unsalted butter until the sauce becomes glossy and slightly thickened.

5. Slice the rested duck breasts diagonally, drizzle with the cherry port sauce, and serve hot. This dish can be served with a side of roasted vegetables, such as roasted potatoes or steamed greens like asparagus or broccoli, to complement the rich flavors of the duck and cherry port sauce.

(per serving): Calories: 450 kcal, 5g, Proteins: 30g, Fats: 25g

Minted Lamb Meatballs

🍴 2 servings 🕐 30 minutes

INGREDIENTS

- 250g (9 oz) ground lamb
- 1/4 cup (30g) breadcrumbs
- 1 small onion, finely chopped
- 2 cloves garlic, minced
- 2 tablespoons chopped fresh mint leaves
- 1 teaspoon dried oregano
- 1 egg
- Salt and pepper to taste
- 2 tablespoons olive oil
- Optional: Greek yogurt for serving

DIRECTIONS

1. In a mixing bowl, combine the ground lamb, breadcrumbs, chopped onion, minced garlic, chopped mint leaves, dried oregano, egg, salt, and pepper. Mix well until all ingredients are thoroughly combined.

2. Form the mixture into meatballs, about 1 to 1.5 inches in diameter.

3. Heat olive oil in a skillet over medium heat. Place the meatballs in the skillet and cook for about 10-12 minutes, turning occasionally, until they are browned and cooked through.

4. Once cooked, transfer the meatballs to a plate lined with paper towels to drain excess oil.

5. Serve the Minted Lamb Meatballs hot, optionally garnished with additional fresh mint leaves and accompanied by a side of Greek yogurt for dipping. These Minted Lamb Meatballs can be served with a side of couscous, rice, or a simple salad tossed with a lemon vinaigrette for a well-rounded meal. They also pair wonderfully with pita bread and tzatziki sauce for a Mediterranean-inspired dish.

(per serving): Calories: 420 kcal, 7g, Proteins: 22g, Fats: 33g

Pork and Pineapple Skewers with Teriyaki Glaze

2 servings | 30 minutes

INGREDIENTS

- 1 cup (225g) pineapple chunks
- 2 tablespoons soy sauce
- 2 tablespoons honey
- 1 tablespoon rice vinegar
- 1 teaspoon minced garlic
- 1/2 teaspoon grated ginger
- 1 tablespoon vegetable oil
- Wooden skewers, soaked in water for 15-20 minutes to prevent burning

DIRECTIONS

1. In a bowl, mix soy sauce, honey, rice vinegar, minced garlic, grated ginger, and vegetable oil to create the teriyaki marinade.

2. Thread the pork cubes and pineapple chunks alternately onto the soaked wooden skewers, distributing them evenly.

3. Place the skewers in a shallow dish and pour half of the teriyaki marinade over them, ensuring they're coated well. Reserve the remaining marinade for later.

4. Preheat the grill or grill pan to medium-high heat. Grill the skewers for about 4-5 minutes per side, brushing them with the reserved teriyaki marinade while cooking, until the pork is cooked through and the pineapple gets grill marks.

5. Once cooked, remove the skewers from the grill and let them rest for a couple of minutes before serving. These Pork and Pineapple Skewers can be served with steamed rice or quinoa and a side of stir-fried vegetables or a fresh green salad for a balanced and satisfying meal.

(per serving): Calories: 320 kcal, 6g, Proteins: 27g, Fats: 12g

MY WEEKLY MEAL PLANNER

Monday

Tuesday

Wednesday

Thursday

Friday

Saturday

Sunday

CHAPTER 12
SMOOTHIE SENSATIONS

Protein-Packed Chocolate Peanut Butter Smoothie

2 servings | 5 minutes

INGREDIENTS

- 2 ripe bananas, frozen
- 2 tablespoons peanut butter
- 2 tablespoons cocoa powder
- 1 cup (240ml) milk (dairy or plant-based)
- 1/2 cup (120g) Greek yogurt
- 1-2 tablespoons honey or maple syrup (optional, for added sweetness)
- 1/2 teaspoon vanilla extract
- 1 cup (150g) ice cubes

DIRECTIONS

1. Place the frozen bananas, peanut butter, cocoa powder, milk, Greek yogurt, honey or maple syrup (if using), vanilla extract, and ice cubes into a blender.

2. Blend on high speed until the mixture is smooth and creamy, scraping down the sides if needed.

3. Pour the Protein-Packed Chocolate Peanut Butter Smoothie into glasses and serve immediately. You can pair it with a handful of nuts, a slice of whole-grain toast with almond butter, or a protein bar for an extra boost of energy and satiety.

(per serving): Calories: 340 kcal, 3g, Proteins: 15g, Fats: 14g

Berry Blast Power Smoothie

🍴 2 servings   🕐 5 minutes

INGREDIENTS

- 1 cup (240ml) unsweetened almond milk (or any preferred milk)
- 1 cup (150g) mixed berries (strawberries, blueberries, raspberries)
- 1 ripe banana, peeled and sliced
- 1/2 cup (120g) Greek yogurt
- 2 tablespoons rolled oats
- 1 tablespoon honey or maple syrup (optional for added sweetness)
- 1 tablespoon chia seeds (optional)
- Ice cubes (as desired)

DIRECTIONS

1. In a blender, combine the almond milk, mixed berries, sliced banana, Greek yogurt, rolled oats, honey (if using), and chia seeds.

2. Blend on high speed until the ingredients are smooth and well combined. If you prefer a thicker consistency, add more ice cubes or frozen berries.

3. Pour the Berry Blast Power Smoothie into glasses and serve immediately.

(per serving): Calories: 220 kcal, Carbohydrates: 45g, Proteins: 7g, Fats: 3g

Coffee Breakfast Smoothie

2 servings | 5 minutes

INGREDIENTS

- 2 ripe bananas, frozen and sliced
- 1 cup (240ml) brewed coffee, cooled
- 1 cup (240ml) milk (dairy or non-dairy)
- 2 tablespoons rolled oats
- 2 tablespoons Greek yogurt
- 1 tablespoon almond butter or peanut butter
- 1 tablespoon honey or maple syrup (optional for sweetness)
- Ice cubes (optional)

DIRECTIONS

1. In a blender, combine the sliced frozen bananas, brewed coffee, milk, rolled oats, Greek yogurt, almond or peanut butter, and honey or maple syrup if using.

2. Blend on high speed until smooth and creamy. If desired, add a few ice cubes and blend again until well incorporated.

3. Taste the smoothie and adjust sweetness or thickness by adding more honey/syrup or liquid as needed.

4. Pour the Coffee Breakfast Smoothie into glasses and serve immediately. This filling smoothie can be served alongside a small breakfast like whole-grain toast with peanut butter or a couple of hard-boiled eggs for a balanced morning meal.

(per serving): Calories: 210 kcal, 37g, Proteins: 6g, Fats: 5g

Green Hulk Smoothie

🍴 2 servings 🕐 5 minutes

INGREDIENTS

- 2 cups (480ml) spinach leaves
- 1 ripe banana, peeled and sliced
- 1 cup (240ml) unsweetened almond milk or any preferred milk
- 1 cup (240ml) Greek yogurt
- 1 tablespoon peanut butter
- 1 tablespoon honey or maple syrup (optional, for sweetness)
- 1/2 cup (75g) frozen pineapple chunks
- 1/2 cup (75g) frozen mango chunks
- 1 tablespoon chia seeds or flaxseeds (optional, for added nutrition)

DIRECTIONS

1. In a blender, combine spinach leaves, sliced banana, almond milk, Greek yogurt, peanut butter, honey (if using), frozen pineapple chunks, frozen mango chunks, and chia or flaxseeds.

2. Blend on high speed until smooth and creamy. If the consistency is too thick, add a bit more almond milk to reach the desired thickness.

3. Pour the Green Hulk Smoothie into glasses and serve immediately. This filling Green Hulk Smoothie can be served as a quick and nutritious breakfast or a post-workout refuel. For added protein, you can pair it with a side of nuts or a slice of whole-grain toast with peanut butter. Enjoy the energizing boost from this nutrient-packed smoothie!

(per serving): Calories: 220 kcal, Carbohydrates: 38g, Proteins: 12g, Fats: 5g

Banana Chocolate Protein Smoothie Bowl

2 servings | 5 minutes

INGREDIENTS

- 2 ripe bananas, frozen and sliced
- 1 cup (240ml) milk (dairy or plant-based)
- 2 tablespoons cocoa powder
- 2 tablespoons peanut butter
- 1 scoop (30g) chocolate protein powder
- Toppings (optional): Sliced bananas, granola, shredded coconut, chia seeds, nuts

DIRECTIONS

1. In a blender, combine the frozen banana slices, milk, cocoa powder, peanut butter, and chocolate protein powder.

2. Blend until smooth and creamy. If the mixture is too thick, you can add a little more milk to reach your desired consistency.

3. Pour the smoothie into bowls.

4. Top the smoothie bowls with sliced bananas, granola, shredded coconut, chia seeds, nuts, or any other desired toppings.

5. Serve immediately and enjoy your Banana Chocolate Protein Smoothie Bowl!

(per serving): Calories: 350 kcal, 6g, Proteins: 20g, Fats: 12g

MY WEEKLY MEAL PLANNER

Monday

Tuesday

Wednesday

Thursday

Friday

Saturday

Sunday

CHAPTER 13
VEGGIE VENTURES

Vegetable Stir-Fry with Tofu

🍴 2 servings 🕒 30 minutes

INGREDIENTS

- 200g (7 oz) firm tofu, cubed
- 2 tablespoons soy sauce
- 1 tablespoon sesame oil
- 1 tablespoon vegetable oil
- 2 cloves garlic, minced
- 1 small onion, sliced
- 1 bell pepper, sliced (any color)
- 1 cup (150g) broccoli florets
- 1 cup (150g) sliced carrots
- 1 cup (150g) snap peas
- Cooked rice or noodles (optional, for serving)

DIRECTIONS

1. Press the tofu between paper towels to remove excess moisture. Cut the tofu into cubes and marinate in soy sauce for about 10 minutes.

2. Heat vegetable oil in a large skillet or wok over medium-high heat. Add the marinated tofu cubes and stir-fry for 5-6 minutes until golden brown. Remove the tofu from the skillet and set aside.

3. In the same skillet, add sesame oil and minced garlic. Stir-fry for a minute until fragrant. Add sliced onions, bell peppers, broccoli florets, sliced carrots, and snap peas. Cook for 4-5 minutes, stirring frequently, until the vegetables are tender yet crisp.

4. Return the cooked tofu to the skillet and toss everything together for an additional minute to heat through.

5. Serve the Vegetable Stir-Fry with Tofu over cooked rice or noodles if desired.

(per serving): Calories: 220 kcal, 5g, Proteins: 14g, Fats: 13g

Zucchini Lasagna

🍴 2 servings   🕐 60 minutes

INGREDIENTS

- 2 medium zucchinis, sliced lengthwise into thin strips
- 1 cup (240ml) marinara sauce
- 1 cup (250g) ricotta cheese
- 1 cup (115g) shredded mozzarella cheese
- 1/2 cup (50g) grated Parmesan cheese
- 1 teaspoon dried basil
- 1 teaspoon dried oregano
- Salt and pepper to taste

DIRECTIONS

1. Preheat your oven to 375°F (190°C). Grease a small baking dish with non-stick spray or olive oil.

2. Lay out the zucchini slices on paper towels and sprinkle them with salt. Let them sit for 10 minutes to draw out excess moisture, then pat them dry with paper towels.

3. In a bowl, mix together the ricotta cheese, half of the shredded mozzarella, half of the grated Parmesan cheese, dried basil, dried oregano, salt, and pepper.

4. Spread a thin layer of marinara sauce on the bottom of the baking dish. Place a layer of zucchini slices on top, slightly overlapping.

5. Spread half of the ricotta cheese mixture over the zucchini slices. Repeat with another layer of marinara sauce, zucchini slices, and the remaining ricotta cheese mixture.

6. Finish with a final layer of marinara sauce and sprinkle the remaining mozzarella and Parmesan cheese on top.

7. Cover the dish with foil and bake for 30 minutes. Then uncover and bake for an additional 15 minutes or until the cheese is bubbly and lightly browned. Zucchini Lasagna can be served with a side salad or garlic bread for a complete meal.

(per serving): Calories: 360 kcal, 5g, Proteins: 28g, Fats: 22g

Sweet Potato and Black Bean Burrito Bowl

2 servings | 35 minutes

INGREDIENTS

- 2 small sweet potatoes, peeled and diced
- 1 can (400g/14 oz) black beans, drained and rinsed
- 1 cup (150g) corn kernels (frozen or canned)
- 1 tablespoon olive oil
- 1 teaspoon chili powder
- 1/2 teaspoon cumin
- 1/2 teaspoon smoked paprika
- Salt and pepper to taste
- Cooked rice (optional, for serving)
- Chopped fresh cilantro or green onions (for garnish)
- Lime wedges (for serving)

DIRECTIONS

1. Preheat the oven to 200°C (400°F). On a baking sheet, toss the diced sweet potatoes with olive oil, chili powder, cumin, smoked paprika, salt, and pepper.

2. Roast the seasoned sweet potatoes in the preheated oven for about 20-25 minutes, or until they are tender and slightly caramelized.

3. In a skillet over medium heat, warm the black beans and corn kernels until heated through. Season with a pinch of chili powder and cumin if desired.

4. To assemble the burrito bowls, divide the cooked rice (if using) between two bowls. Top each with roasted sweet potatoes, black bean and corn mixture, and any additional desired toppings like chopped cilantro or green onions.

5. Serve the Sweet Potato and Black Bean Burrito Bowls with lime wedges on the side for an added citrus kick. They can also be served with a side of tortilla chips, guacamole, or a dollop of Greek yogurt for extra creaminess and a boost of protein

(per serving): Calories: 320 kcal, 60g, Proteins: 12g, Fats: 5g

Cauliflower Steak with Chimichurri

🍴 2 servings 🕐 30 minutes

INGREDIENTS

- 1 large head of cauliflower
- 2 tablespoons olive oil
- Salt and black pepper to taste

Chimichurri Sauce:
- 1 cup (240ml) fresh parsley, finely chopped
- 3 cloves garlic, minced
- 2 tablespoons red wine vinegar
- 4 tablespoons olive oil
- 1 tablespoon fresh lemon juice
- 1/2 teaspoon red pepper flakes (optional)
- Salt and pepper to taste

DIRECTIONS

1. Preheat the oven to 425°F (220°C). Line a baking sheet with parchment paper.

2. Remove the leaves from the cauliflower and trim the stem end to create a flat base. Slice the cauliflower into 1-inch thick "steaks."

3. Place the cauliflower steaks on the prepared baking sheet. Brush both sides with olive oil and season with salt and pepper.

4. Roast the cauliflower in the preheated oven for about 15-20 minutes, flipping halfway through, until golden brown and tender.

5. Meanwhile, prepare the chimichurri sauce. In a bowl, mix together finely chopped parsley, minced garlic, red wine vinegar, olive oil, lemon juice, red pepper flakes (if using), salt, and pepper. Adjust seasoning to taste.

6. Once the cauliflower steaks are cooked, serve them hot, drizzled generously with chimichurri sauce. This can also be served with a side of roasted potatoes, a quinoa salad, or even alongside a simple green salad for a well-rounded and satisfying meal.

(per serving): Calories: 220 kcal, 12g, Proteins: 4g, Fats: 18g

Grilled Veggie Tacos with Avocado Cream

🍴 2 servings   🕐 30 minutes

INGREDIENTS

For the Grilled Veggies:
- 2 large bell peppers (any color), sliced
- 1 large zucchini, sliced lengthwise
- 1 small red onion, sliced
- 1 tablespoon olive oil
- 1 teaspoon chili powder
- 1/2 teaspoon cumin
- Salt and pepper to taste

For the Avocado Cream:
- 1 ripe avocado
- 1/4 cup (60ml) Greek yogurt
- Juice of 1 lime
- Salt to taste

For Serving:
- 4-6 small tortillas
- Fresh cilantro (optional, for garnish)
- Lime wedges (for serving)

DIRECTIONS

1. Preheat your grill or grill pan over medium-high heat. Toss sliced bell peppers, zucchini, and red onion in olive oil, chili powder, cumin, salt, and pepper.

2. Grill the seasoned veggies for about 5-7 minutes per side until they are tender and have grill marks.

3. Meanwhile, prepare the avocado cream. In a blender or food processor, combine the avocado, Greek yogurt, lime juice, and salt. Blend until smooth and creamy. Adjust seasoning to taste.

4. Warm the tortillas on the grill for about 20-30 seconds per side.

5. Assemble the tacos by placing a generous amount of grilled veggies on each tortilla. Drizzle with avocado cream and garnish with fresh cilantro if desired. Serve with lime wedges. These can also be served with a side of Mexican rice, black beans, or a simple corn salad to make a complete and satisfying meal.

(per serving): Calories: 320 kcal, 35g, Proteins: 8g, Fats: 18g

MY WEEKLY MEAL PLANNER

Monday

Tuesday

Wednesday

Thursday

Friday

Saturday

Sunday

CHAPTER 14
SAUCES, DIPS & DRESSINGS

Cilantro-Lime Crema

2 servings | 5 minutes

INGREDIENTS

- 1/2 cup (120ml) sour cream
- 2 tablespoons (30ml) mayonnaise
- 2 tablespoons (30ml) freshly squeezed lime juice
- Zest of 1 lime
- 2 tablespoons (8g) chopped fresh cilantro
- 1 clove garlic, minced
- Salt and pepper to taste

DIRECTIONS

1. In a mixing bowl, combine sour cream, mayonnaise, lime juice, lime zest, chopped cilantro, minced garlic, salt, and pepper. Mix well until all ingredients are thoroughly combined.

2. Taste and adjust seasoning if needed. If you prefer a thinner consistency, you can add a little bit of water or lime juice to achieve your desired thickness.

3. Transfer the Cilantro-Lime Crema to a serving bowl or container. It's now ready to be served or stored in the refrigerator for later use. This zesty and creamy Cilantro-Lime Crema can be served as a versatile dip for tortilla chips, a flavorful sauce for tacos, burritos, or grilled meats, or as a topping for salads or nachos.

(per serving): Calories: 120 kcal, 2g, Proteins: 1g, Fats: 12g

Guacamole

🍴 2 servings   🕐 10 minutes

INGREDIENTS

- 2 ripe avocados
- 1/2 small red onion, finely chopped
- 1 small tomato, diced
- 1/4 cup (15g) fresh cilantro, chopped
- Juice of 1 lime
- Salt and pepper to taste

DIRECTIONS

1. Cut the avocados in half, remove the pits, and scoop the flesh into a bowl.

2. Mash the avocado with a fork, leaving some chunks for texture.

3. Add chopped red onion, diced tomato, chopped cilantro, lime juice, salt, and pepper. Mix until well combined.

4. Taste and adjust seasoning if needed. Serve the Guacamole immediately with tortilla chips or use as a topping for tacos, burritos, or nachos.

(per serving): Calories: 240 kcal, 15g, Proteins: 3g, Fats: 22g

Corn and Black Bean Salsa

2 servings | 10 minutes

INGREDIENTS

- 1 can (400g/14 oz) black beans, drained and rinsed
- 1 cup (150g) sweet corn kernels (fresh, canned, or frozen)
- 1 small red bell pepper, diced
- 1 small red onion, finely chopped
- 1 jalapeño pepper, seeded and finely chopped
- 1/4 cup (60ml) fresh lime juice (approximately 2-3 limes)
- 2 tablespoons chopped fresh cilantro (coriander)
- 1 teaspoon ground cumin
- Salt and pepper to taste

DIRECTIONS

1. In a mixing bowl, combine the black beans, sweet corn kernels, diced red bell pepper, finely chopped red onion, and seeded and chopped jalapeño pepper.

2. Add fresh lime juice, chopped cilantro, ground cumin, salt, and pepper to the bowl. Mix well until all ingredients are evenly combined.

3. Taste and adjust seasoning if needed. For more spice, add additional jalapeño or a pinch of red pepper flakes.

4. Allow the flavors to meld together by refrigerating the Corn and Black Bean Salsa for at least 30 minutes before serving. This flavorful salsa can be served with tortilla chips as a dip or used as a topping for tacos, burritos, grilled chicken, or fish.

(per serving): Calories: 180 kcal, Carbohydrates: 35g, Proteins: 10g, Fats: 1g

Tangy Thousand Island Dressing

🍴 2 servings 🕐 10 minutes

INGREDIENTS

- 120 ml (1/2 cup) mayonnaise
- 30 ml (2 tablespoons) ketchup
- 15 ml (1 tablespoon) sweet pickle relish
- 5 ml (1 teaspoon) white vinegar
- 2.5 ml (1/2 teaspoon) granulated sugar
- 1.25 ml (1/4 teaspoon) onion powder
- Salt and pepper to taste

DIRECTIONS

1. In a small mixing bowl, combine the mayonnaise, ketchup, sweet pickle relish, white vinegar, granulated sugar, onion powder, salt, and pepper.

2. Whisk the ingredients together until well combined and smooth.

3. Taste the dressing and adjust seasoning, adding more salt, pepper, or sugar if desired.

4. Transfer the Thousand Island Dressing to a jar or airtight container and refrigerate until ready to serve. It can be used as a salad dressing, burger or sandwich spread, or as a dipping sauce for veggies or chicken tenders.

(per serving): Calories: 170 kcal, ... g, Proteins: 0 g, Fats: 16 g

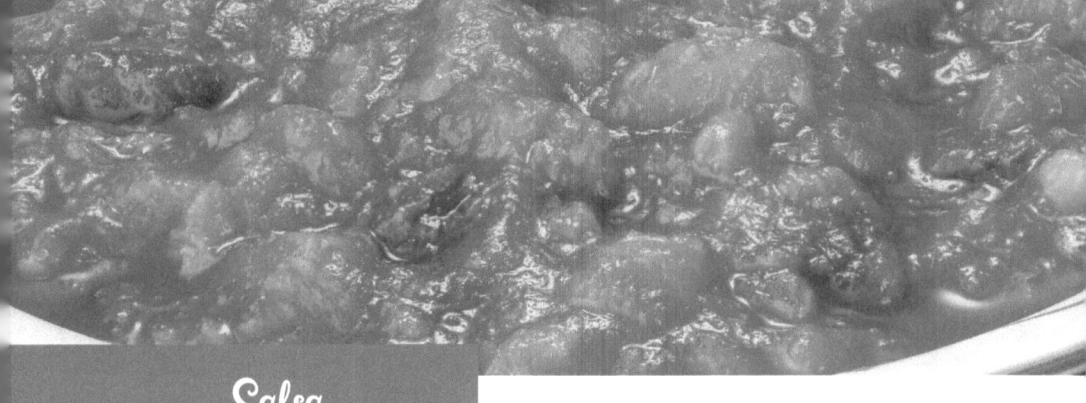

Salsa

🍴 2 servings 🕐 10 minutes

INGREDIENTS

- 2 medium tomatoes, diced
- 1/4 cup (40g) red onion, finely chopped
- 1/4 cup (15g) fresh cilantro, chopped
- 1 jalapeño or chili pepper, seeded and finely chopped (optional for heat)
- Juice of 1 lime
- Salt and pepper to taste

DIRECTIONS

1. In a bowl, combine diced tomatoes, chopped red onion, chopped cilantro, and finely chopped jalapeño or chili pepper (if using).

2. Squeeze the lime juice over the mixture and season with salt and pepper. Stir until well combined.

3. Taste and adjust seasoning if needed. Serve the Salsa immediately with tortilla chips, or use as a topping for tacos, quesadillas, or grilled meats.

(per serving): Calories: 25 kcal, 6g, Proteins: 1g, Fats: 0g

Creamy Alfredo Sauce

🍴 2 servings   🕐 15 minutes

INGREDIENTS

- 1/4 cup (56g) unsalted butter
- 2 cloves garlic, minced
- 1 cup (240ml) heavy cream
- 1 cup (100g) grated Parmesan cheese
- Salt and black pepper to taste
- Fresh parsley or basil for garnish (optional)

DIRECTIONS

1. In a saucepan over medium-low heat, melt the unsalted butter. Add the minced garlic and cook for 1-2 minutes until fragrant, stirring occasionally.

2. Pour in the heavy cream, stirring continuously. Bring the mixture to a gentle simmer, but avoid boiling.

3. Gradually add the grated Parmesan cheese while stirring constantly until the cheese melts and the sauce thickens, about 3-5 minutes. Be careful not to let the sauce boil.

4. Season the Alfredo sauce with salt and black pepper to taste. Continue stirring until the sauce reaches your desired thickness.

5. Remove the sauce from heat. Serve the Creamy Alfredo Sauce over cooked pasta such as fettuccine, spaghetti, or penne. . It can also be used as a sauce for chicken or served over vegetables for a hearty and filling meal.

(per serving): Calories: 500 kcal, 5g, Proteins: 15g, Fats: 46g

Homemade Basil Pesto Sauce

2 servings | 10 minutes

INGREDIENTS

- 2 cups (60g) fresh basil leaves, packed
- 1/3 cup (40g) pine nuts or walnuts
- 1/3 cup (25g) grated Parmesan cheese
- 2 cloves garlic, peeled
- 1/2 cup (120ml) extra-virgin olive oil
- Salt and pepper to taste

DIRECTIONS

1. In a food processor or blender, combine the basil leaves, pine nuts or walnuts, grated Parmesan cheese, and peeled garlic cloves.

2. Pulse the ingredients while slowly drizzling in the extra-virgin olive oil until the mixture reaches a smooth consistency. Add more olive oil if needed to achieve the desired texture.

3. Season the pesto sauce with salt and pepper to taste. Blend once more to incorporate the seasoning evenly.

4. Serve the Homemade Basil Pesto Sauce immediately or store it in an airtight container in the refrigerator for up to a week. This flavorful Basil Pesto Sauce can be served with pasta, spread on sandwiches, used as a dip for bread, mixed into salads, or as a topping for grilled chicken or fish.

(per serving): Calories: 480 kcal, 2g, Proteins: 6g, Fats: 50g

MY WEEKLY MEAL PLANNER

Monday

Tuesday

Wednesday

Thursday

Friday

Saturday

Sunday

CONCLUSION

Hey there, champs!

Congratulations on reaching the end of my cookbook journey designed especially for you—yes, YOU, the college culinary wizards in the making!

So, did you enjoy the flavorful ride through these pages? Did your taste buds do a happy dance with our recipes? Now, spill the beans - what was your absolute favorite recipe? The one that made you do a little victory dance in the kitchen? Give me a virtual thumbs up if you've found your new favorite dish!

From quick bites to belly-filling meals, I've dished out a parade of flavors, ensuring each recipe is as easy to conquer as acing that last-minute cram session.

Let's flip through the highlight reel: Breakfast wonders, sidekicks for your main courses, salads that go "POW" in your mouth, and sauces that scream "DELICIOUSNESS!" You name it, I've served it up with a side of fun and a sprinkle of kitchen magic. It's been an incredible journey to navigate the bachelor's kitchen, armed with spatulas and a sprinkle of culinary magic.

A huge "THANK YOU" from the bottom of my mixing bowls for joining this flavorful expedition. I hope these recipes not only filled your tummies but also added some spice to your college days.

As you venture forth, conquering the kitchen and your academic pursuits, here's wishing you culinary triumphs, study success, and memorable dinner dates!

Before we sign off, I'd love to hear your thoughts! Your feedback is my secret sauce for cooking up even more awesome content. So, drop me a line, share your reviews, and let me know what other kitchen adventures you'd love to explore!

Until next time, keep those pots stirring, those ovens baking, and those taste buds tingling! Bon appétit and happy cooking, fellow kitchen legends!

Made in United States
Troutdale, OR
01/21/2024